FORGIVING WHAT YOU CANT FORGET

A Practical Guide on How To Heal, Forgive The Past and move on, Make Peace With Painful Relationships and Overcome Your Emotional Wounds

LYSA MOREEN

1

TABLE OF CONTENT

3.3 Releasing Emotional Baggage: Letting Go of
Unresolved Grief
3.4 Embracing Vulnerability: Finding Strength in
Your Woundedness

Chapter 4: Cultivating Compassion

4.1 The Art of Empathy: Connecting with Others'
Pain
4.2 Breaking Barriers: Overcoming Obstacles to
Empathy
4.3 Compassion for Self: Treating Yourself with
Kindness
4.4 Choosing Forgiveness: Discovering the
Freedom of Compassionate Release

**Chapter 5: The Healing Power of Self-
Forgiveness**

5.1 Self-Compassion: Offering Yourself
Forgiveness
5.2 Learning from Mistakes: Transforming Regret
into Growth
5.3 Healing Inner Wounds: Nurturing Your Inner
Child
5.4 The Liberation of Self-Forgiveness: Releasing
Guilt and Shame

Chapter 6: Navigating Difficult Relationships

6.1 Understanding Toxicity: Identifying Harmful
Relationships

Chapter 13: Embracing a Life of Forgiveness

Conclusion

Introduction

In the depths of my soul, I once carried a heavy burden of pain and betrayal, inflicted upon me by those I trusted most. The world felt wicked and unyielding, as I grappled with the weight of past wrongs, unable to move forward. My heart was trapped in a cycle of resentment, and the wounds seemed too deep to ever heal. It was a place of darkness where forgiveness seemed like an unattainable dream.

As days turned into years, I carried this emotional baggage, lugging it around like an anchor. Every attempt to break free seemed futile, leaving me feeling lost and defeated. The people I had loved had hurt me, and I couldn't fathom how to forgive, let alone forget. It was in this darkness that I realized the immense power of pain, and how it had become the driving force in my life.

Yet, amidst the shadows, there was a glimmer of hope. A light that beckoned me to embark on a path of healing and transformation. It was a whisper of possibility that inspired me to take a step towards letting go of the past and finding peace within myself.

Through countless soul-searching moments, I learned that forgiveness wasn't a gift I gave to those who wronged me; it was a gift I bestowed upon myself. It wasn't about condoning the hurtful actions of others, but about freeing myself from the chains of resentment. It was an act of courage, strength, and self-love, a profound realization that I could control my response to the pain inflicted upon me.

I navigated the labyrinth of my emotions, confronting my wounds, and slowly dismantling the fortress of bitterness I had built around my heart. It was a journey that demanded vulnerability, as I faced the depths of my own pain with an open heart, embracing compassion for both myself and those who had hurt me.

As I walked this path of healing, I discovered the transformative power of forgiveness. It was the key that unlocked the door to liberation, offering me a renewed sense of empowerment and resilience. I began to see the world through a different lens, not denying its imperfections, but choosing to respond with grace and understanding.

Today, I stand before you as living proof that healing is possible, even in the face of unimaginable pain. The wounds may still leave scars, but they no longer dictate my journey. I have found a way to move on and rebuild my life, guided by the wisdom of forgiveness and the strength of my experiences.

In writing this book, I aim to share my personal narrative, as a beacon of hope for those who find themselves trapped in the darkness of their past. Through my story, I hope to inspire and empower readers to embark on their own journeys of healing, to forgive what they couldn't forget, and to embrace a life of wholeness and compassion.

May my experiences serve as a guide, reminding you that even in the darkest moments, there lies the potential for growth and transformation. Together, let us embark on a path towards healing, forgiveness, and the profound freedom that comes with letting go of what once held us captive.

CHAPTER 1

Forgiveness

In the depths of my despair, forgiveness seemed like an impossible task. The pain inflicted by those I trusted had wounded me to the core, leaving scars that seemed to define my very existence. Bitterness and resentment had become my constant companions, weighing down my heart and clouding my perception of the world.

As I stood at the crossroads of my emotions, contemplating the path forward, a voice within me whispered the transformative power of forgiveness. It was a concept I struggled to grasp, for I believed forgiving those who wronged me would diminish the significance of their hurtful actions. However, as I embarked on this journey, I discovered that forgiveness wasn't a gift I bestowed upon others; it was a profound act of self-love and liberation.

Forgiveness was my key to emotional freedom. It didn't mean erasing the memories or excusing the pain; instead, it allowed me to release the shackles of resentment and embrace the power of choice. I could choose to free myself from the emotional prison I had built, choosing a path of healing and growth.

Opening my heart to forgiveness was like unlocking a hidden reservoir of strength within me. It required courage to confront my emotions head-on, to face the pain that had haunted me for so long. Yet, as I took the first step towards letting go, I felt an immense weight lift off my shoulders. The burden of anger and bitterness began to dissolve, making way for a sense of lightness and clarity.

Through forgiveness, I realized that healing was not about forgetting the past, but rather, transforming my relationship with it. I acknowledged that the scars would remain, but they didn't have to dictate my future. By granting forgiveness, I reclaimed control over my life, no longer allowing the actions of others to define my happiness.

In the process, I also learned that forgiveness was not a linear journey. There were moments of doubt and relapses into old patterns of resentment. But through self-compassion and patience, I embraced the setbacks as part of my growth. I reminded myself that healing was a process, and it was okay to stumble along the way.

As I unraveled the layers of my emotions, I discovered an unexpected gift within forgiveness - empathy. By recognizing the humanity in those who had hurt me, I saw the complexities of their own pain and struggles. This newfound empathy didn't excuse their actions, but it allowed me to break free from the cycle of victimhood.

With each step towards forgiveness, I felt a renewed sense of empowerment. I realized that I held the power to define my emotional well-being, regardless of the circumstances. I no longer allowed past wounds to dictate my present and future. Instead, I chose to embrace my capacity to heal and grow beyond the pain.

In embracing forgiveness, I learned that it wasn't just about others; it was about freeing myself from the chains of resentment. It was an act of self-love, self-compassion, and a deep commitment to my own healing. The power to forgive was within me all along, waiting to be unleashed and guide me towards emotional freedom.

The Psychology of Letting Go: Breaking Free from Resentment

With the newfound power of forgiveness, I looked deeper into the psychology of letting go. I had come to understand that holding onto resentment was akin to gripping onto a hot coal, expecting the other person to be burned. In reality, it only consumed me from within, leaving scars that perpetuated the pain.

Letting go was a profound act of liberation. It meant relinquishing the need to hold others accountable for my emotional well-being. As I explored the intricacies of this process, I discovered that letting go didn't mean forgetting or excusing the hurtful actions; rather, it meant choosing to release the emotional grip they had on me.

In the past, I had clung to resentment as a form of protection, a shield to prevent further harm. But in doing so, I also denied myself the opportunity to heal and grow. I had to confront my fear of vulnerability, allowing myself to be emotionally exposed and trusting that I could navigate the pain with resilience.

The process of letting go required me to confront my own triggers and traumas. I had to recognize that my reactions were not solely a result of the present situation but were also intertwined with past wounds. This awareness allowed me to respond from a place of mindfulness rather than react from a place of unresolved pain.

As I practiced letting go, I faced resistance from within. My mind would replay past events, reigniting the flames of anger and hurt. But I reminded myself that I had the power to choose my response. I could either dwell in the darkness of resentment or embrace the light of healing and forgiveness.

Letting go also involved setting boundaries with those who had caused me pain. It was not an act of punishment but a means of self-preservation. I had to prioritize my well-being and ensure that I was surrounded by healthy and supportive relationships.

In breaking free from resentment, I learned to forgive not just others but also myself. I embraced the imperfections within me and allowed myself the grace to heal from past mistakes. Self-forgiveness was a vital aspect of the healing journey, acknowledging that I too deserved compassion and understanding.

As I progressed on this path, I noticed a profound shift in my perspective. The world no longer seemed as wicked as it once did. Instead, I saw it through a lens of empathy and understanding. I recognized that everyone carried their own burdens and wounds, and it was not my place to judge them.

Letting go didn't mean erasing the past; it meant embracing the present with an open heart. It meant finding freedom in forgiveness, in releasing the grip of bitterness, and in choosing to respond with love and compassion. This journey of letting go empowered me to create a future filled with peace and emotional liberation.

Embracing Imperfection: Learning to Forgive Yourself

In my quest for healing and forgiveness, I faced a daunting challenge - learning to forgive myself. The weight of my own mistakes and perceived inadequacies had woven a web of guilt and shame, entangling my heart and soul. It was easier to forgive others than to extend that same compassion to myself.

I had always been my harshest critic, berating myself for every misstep and failure. The wounds inflicted by others seemed to pale in comparison to the wounds I had self-inflicted. In the pursuit of perfection, I had lost touch with my own humanity, denying myself the very grace and understanding I offered to others.

As I stood at the precipice of self-forgiveness, I realized that healing began within. It was time to break free from the illusion of perfection and embrace my imperfections with kindness and acceptance. This was not an easy task, as it required confronting deep-rooted beliefs about my worthiness and lovability.

I embarked on a journey of self-discovery, exploring the reasons behind my relentless self-criticism. Unearthing these beliefs was painful, but it allowed me to challenge their validity. I began to understand that I was deserving of forgiveness and compassion, just as every human being was. I was imperfect, just like everyone else, and that was okay.

As I started to embrace imperfection, I discovered a newfound sense of freedom. I no longer needed to carry the burden of self-condemnation. I recognized that making mistakes was a natural part of the human experience, and they were opportunities for growth and learning.

Self-forgiveness required me to let go of the past versions of myself that I clung to with regret. I needed to accept that I had changed and evolved, and that my worth was not determined by my past actions. It was a process of releasing myself from the chains of shame and stepping into a future of self-compassion.

With each act of self-forgiveness, I felt a sense of self-empowerment. I realized that I held the pen to my life's narrative, and I could rewrite the story of my self-worth. I chose to define myself by my resilience and ability to grow from my mistakes, rather than be bound by the shadows of my past.

Embracing imperfection was a continuous practice. There were days when self-doubt would creep in, attempting to sabotage my progress. But I reminded myself that self-forgiveness was not a destination; it was a lifelong journey of self-discovery and self-love.

In my pursuit of healing and self-forgiveness, I also found the courage to extend forgiveness to those who had wronged me. Embracing my own imperfections allowed me to recognize the humanity in others and their capacity for growth and change. I no longer clung to resentment towards them, but instead, I offered them the same compassion I had learned to give myself.

The journey of forgiving myself was intertwined with forgiving others. It was a reminder that we were all imperfect beings on our own unique paths of growth and understanding. It was a realization that compassion, both for ourselves and others, was the gateway to emotional liberation.

As I embraced self-forgiveness, I also discovered the strength to set healthy boundaries in my relationships. I no longer allowed others to define my worth or dictate my emotional well-being. Instead, I honored my boundaries and prioritized my own happiness.

In learning to forgive myself, I found the key to unlocking my own emotional freedom. It was a transformative process of self-discovery, compassion, and acceptance. Through self-forgiveness, I learned that I was worthy of love and understanding, and that I held the power to create a life filled with joy and emotional wholeness.

The Journey to Healing: Navigating the Path of Forgiveness

The journey to healing through forgiveness was not a straight path but a winding road filled with twists and turns. It required courage, vulnerability, and unwavering commitment to my own growth. Along this path, I encountered moments of doubt and uncertainty, but I held onto the light of hope that guided me towards emotional liberation.

As I navigated this journey, I discovered the importance of self-compassion. I learned to be gentle with myself when I stumbled or faltered. Instead of chastising myself for not healing fast enough, I reminded myself that healing was a process, and it was okay to take my time. I allowed myself the space to feel and process my emotions, without judgment or self-criticism.

In the pursuit of healing, I also sought support from trusted friends and loved ones. Sharing my journey with them was both humbling and empowering. They became my pillars of strength, offering a safe space for me to be vulnerable and authentic. Their encouragement and understanding provided the validation I needed to continue on this path.

I also sought guidance from professional counselors and therapists. They helped me delve deeper into my emotions, providing valuable insights and tools to navigate the complexities of forgiveness. Through therapy, I learned healthy coping mechanisms and communication skills that facilitated my healing journey.

One of the most significant lessons I learned on this path was the power of gratitude. As I embraced forgiveness and healing, I found myself grateful for the lessons that pain had taught me. I recognized that my struggles had shaped me into a stronger, more compassionate person. I was grateful for the opportunity to grow and evolve beyond my past wounds.

The journey to healing through forgiveness was not just about the destination but the transformation that occurred along the way. I discovered strength and resilience I never knew I possessed. I recognized that forgiveness was not a one-time event but a continuous practice that required nurturing and commitment.

Through forgiveness, I also found the courage to reclaim my narrative. I was no longer defined by my past or the actions of others. Instead, I became the author of my own story, creating a future built on love, compassion, and self-empowerment.

As I embraced forgiveness, I also became aware of the interconnectedness of all beings. My healing journey inspired me to extend compassion not only to those who had wronged me but to all living beings. I saw the potential for growth and transformation in each individual, and I strived to be a beacon of light and understanding in a world that sorely needed it.

The journey to healing through forgiveness was not without its challenges. There were moments of darkness and doubt, but I held onto the flicker of hope within me. I learned to trust in the process of healing, knowing that each step, no matter how small, brought me closer to emotional liberation.

As I stand here now, reflecting on my journey, I am filled with gratitude for the path I have walked. The wounds that once defined me are now a testament to my resilience and capacity for growth. Through forgiveness, I have discovered the true meaning of emotional freedom - a freedom that comes from within and cannot be taken away by external circumstances.

In sharing my story, I hope to inspire you, to embark on your own journey of healing and forgiveness. It may not be easy, and there will be moments of uncertainty, but know that you are not alone. The power to heal and forgive lies within you, waiting to be unleashed.

May you find the courage to confront your pain, the strength to embrace imperfection, and the wisdom to navigate the path of forgiveness. May you discover the transformative power of forgiveness and the profound freedom that comes with letting go of what you couldn't forget.

Remember, healing is not an endpoint; it is an ongoing journey of growth and self-discovery. Embrace the challenges, celebrate the victories, and above all, be kind to yourself. You are worthy of love, compassion, and forgiveness - both from others and, most importantly, from yourself.

In forgiveness, may you find the key to unlocking the door to your own emotional liberation and embrace a life of wholeness and peace. May you find the strength to forgive what you couldn't forget and move forward on your path of healing and empowerment.

CHAPTER 2

Confronting Emotional Wounds

Acknowledging Pain: The First Step to Healing

In this journey of healing, the first crucial step is to acknowledge the pain that resides within you. For too long, you may have buried your emotions, pushing them deep down, hoping they would disappear. But remember, healing begins with accepting the reality of your feelings.

You may have experienced hurt, betrayal, or heartbreak from trusted individuals, leaving emotional wounds that seem insurmountable. It's okay to feel overwhelmed or confused, for these emotions are valid. In the depths of your vulnerability, you find the strength to confront the pain head-on, and by doing so, you embark on the path of healing.

Allow yourself the time and space to sit with your emotions, for they hold the key to understanding your inner world. Feel the weight of the hurt, the rawness of the wounds, and know that it is okay to feel this way. Acknowledging your pain does not make you weak; instead, it signifies your courage to confront your truth.

In this process, you might encounter resistance or fear, questioning whether you have the strength to face the intensity of your emotions. Know that it's okay to be hesitant; healing is not an overnight journey. Take one step at a time, granting yourself the compassion and patience needed to navigate this uncharted territory.

As you begin to open the door to your emotional landscape, you'll find the wounds you've long suppressed start to surface. Memories, both vivid and faded, may resurface, triggering an array of emotions. Embrace these moments with gentleness, as they signify the emergence of buried emotions seeking acknowledgment.

Remember, you are not alone in this process. Seek support from loved ones, or even professional guidance if needed. Sometimes, sharing your pain with someone you trust can provide a sense of relief and validation. This support system can be your beacon of hope during times of vulnerability.

By taking the courageous step to acknowledge your pain, you set the foundation for a transformative healing journey. It's like tending to a garden; before planting new seeds of growth, you must first clear the weeds and till the soil. In the same way, acknowledging your pain prepares the ground for nurturing the seeds of healing and forgiveness.

Unearthing Past Hurts: Dealing with Buried Emotions

Buried emotions are like forgotten treasures, hidden away in the recesses of your heart and mind. They hold the remnants of past experiences, both joyful and traumatic, shaping your emotional landscape. Unearthing these emotions requires a willingness to confront the shadows of your past, but it is through this excavation that you uncover invaluable insights into your own inner world.

During this phase, you may come across memories you thought were long forgotten, resurfacing with surprising clarity. These recollections might be associated with moments of joy, love, or laughter, reminding you of the depth of your emotional capacity. Conversely, you might also encounter memories of pain, betrayal, or abandonment, evoking a range of emotions from anger to sorrow.

It's crucial to approach this process with compassion for yourself, recognizing that buried emotions might feel overwhelming. You might find yourself entangled in a web of conflicting emotions, unsure of how to navigate them. But remember, it's okay to feel and experience these emotions. They are a part of your healing journey.

As you unearth these emotions, you might also start to notice patterns in your emotional responses. Repetitive negative patterns may have been formed as a defense mechanism to shield yourself from further pain. However, these patterns can become barriers to healing and growth, as they often prevent you from fully embracing forgiveness and moving forward.

Confronting these patterns can be challenging, but it is an essential step in breaking free from their hold on your life. Recognize the triggers that ignite these patterns and explore their origin. Understanding their roots empowers you to dismantle them, creating space for healthier emotional responses.

In the process of unearthing past hurts, you may question the validity of your emotions, wondering if you have the right to feel hurt or angry. Remember, dear reader, your feelings are valid, regardless of what others may say or how they may perceive them. Honor your emotions without judgment, for they are a reflection of your unique human experience.

As you journey through this process, you might discover layers of emotions that have been suppressed for a long time. Embrace this emergence, as it signifies your willingness to face the truth and grant yourself the freedom to heal.

With each layer unearthed, you inch closer to the core of your pain, where genuine healing resides.

During this phase, self-compassion becomes your closest ally. Treat yourself with the same kindness you would offer a dear friend. Embrace the wounded parts of yourself with love and understanding, and let them know they are safe to be seen and acknowledged.

Breaking the Cycle: Overcoming Repetitive Negative Patterns

As you journey through the labyrinth of healing, you come face to face with the cycle of behaviors and responses that have held you captive for far too long.

Repetitive negative patterns are like well-worn paths, etched into your subconscious mind through past experiences. These patterns often manifest as defensive mechanisms or coping strategies that once served to protect you from harm. However, over time, they may have become obstacles, hindering your ability to heal and forgive.

Recognizing these patterns is the first step in dismantling them. You might find yourself reacting in certain ways to specific triggers, falling into the same emotional pitfalls time and again. These patterns can manifest in various aspects of your life, from personal relationships to how you handle stress and adversity.

Breaking free from these patterns requires mindfulness and self-awareness. Begin by observing your thoughts, feelings, and actions without judgment. Notice the recurring themes that emerge during times of emotional intensity. Identifying these patterns helps you gain insight into the underlying beliefs and emotions driving them.

Once you recognize the patterns, it's time to challenge their validity. Ask yourself if these responses still serve your growth and well-being. Are they helping you move towards forgiveness and healing, or are they keeping you stuck in the past? As you question their purpose, you empower yourself to rewrite the narrative of your emotional journey.

At times, breaking the cycle might require seeking support from a professional or confiding in a trusted friend or loved one. Speaking about your experiences and emotions can provide you with a fresh perspective and valuable insights. Remember that you don't have to navigate this journey alone; there is strength in vulnerability and seeking help when needed.

As you actively work towards breaking the cycle, you may encounter moments of resistance or relapse. Old habits can be deeply ingrained, and slipping back into familiar patterns is normal. Be gentle with yourself during these times, acknowledging that healing is not linear. Each step forward, no matter how small, is progress towards your liberation.

Along this journey, you'll also learn the art of validation and the power of honoring your feelings. Sometimes, you might have dismissed your emotions, telling yourself they were unwarranted or unimportant. However, each emotion you experience is valid, and by acknowledging them, you honor your authentic self.

Embrace the full spectrum of your emotions, even the ones that might seem uncomfortable or difficult to process. They all play a part in your healing journey. By validating your feelings, you give yourself permission to heal and to find peace with your past.

As you continue to break the cycle of repetitive negative patterns, you'll notice a gradual shift in your emotional landscape. New paths of self-awareness and empowerment emerge, leading you towards the transformative power of forgiveness. The more you practice breaking these patterns, the closer you move towards the freedom to heal and forgive.

Honoring Your Feelings: Validating Your Emotional Experience

Honoring your feelings begins with acknowledging that they are an essential part of who you are. Emotions are a natural response to life's experiences, and they carry valuable information about your needs, desires, and boundaries. Embrace the complexity of your emotions, for they reflect the richness of your human experience.

When you encounter moments of sadness, anger, or fear, do not suppress or dismiss them. Instead, sit with these emotions and observe them without judgment. Understand that they are messengers, communicating what your heart needs at that particular moment. By paying attention to your feelings, you open yourself up to a deeper connection with your inner self.

Validating your emotional experience is a radical act of self-love. It involves accepting your feelings as valid, regardless of external judgments or expectations. Remember that you have the right to feel what you feel, and your emotions are worthy of acknowledgement.

You might come across people who invalidate your emotions, claiming that you should "just get over it" or "move on." Do not let their words diminish the significance of your feelings. Instead, surround yourself with individuals who offer genuine support and understanding, uplifting you during times of emotional vulnerability.

By honoring and validating your feelings, you create an emotional safe space within yourself. This safe space becomes a sanctuary where you can express yourself authentically, without the fear of judgment. It is in this sanctuary that healing begins to blossom, as you nurture the wounded parts of yourself with love and acceptance.

Remember that healing is not a linear process. There might be days when your emotions feel overwhelming, and that's okay. Allow yourself to feel whatever arises without resisting or forcing it away. Embrace the ebb and flow of your emotional journey, knowing that each wave carries the potential for transformation.

As you continue to honor and validate your emotional experience, you'll notice a subtle shift in how you respond to your emotions. Instead of suppressing or denying them, you'll develop healthier coping strategies to navigate through challenging moments. You'll cultivate resilience, recognizing that emotions are not permanent states but passing clouds in the sky of your consciousness.

Through this transformative process, you'll gain a deeper understanding of yourself and your emotional landscape. You'll come to realize that your feelings are not your identity but a part of the vast and ever-changing tapestry of your being. This newfound awareness allows you to detach from the grip of your past and step into the present moment with greater clarity.

CHAPTER 3

Unraveling the Past

Reflecting on the Past: Gaining Clarity on Your Story

In our hearts, we all carry memories of the past, some filled with joy and laughter, while others are shrouded in pain and betrayal. When we find ourselves unable to move on, it is essential to embark on a journey of reflection to gain clarity on our stories. So, take a deep breath, dear reader, and let us delve into the healing power of self-discovery.

As you access your emotions, you might find it daunting to confront the memories that haunt you. But remember, it is only by facing them head-on that you can begin to understand their hold over you. Acknowledge that it's okay to feel overwhelmed; this process takes time and requires gentle self-compassion.

You might be tempted to bury the painful memories, hoping they will fade away with time. However, avoiding the past only prolongs your healing journey. Instead, allow yourself to sit with these memories, gently exploring the emotions they evoke. Embrace vulnerability and open your heart to the hurt you carry within, for it is through this act of courage that you can start to unravel the tangled threads of your past.

In the midst of reflection, you may encounter moments of resistance or fear. Perhaps you fear that facing the past will consume you, leaving you trapped in a sea of sorrow. Yet, remember that you are not alone on this journey. Seek support from loved ones, a trusted friend, or a professional guide who can walk beside you, providing solace and understanding.

With each step you take, you will gain insight into the patterns that shaped your responses and relationships. You'll start to see how past experiences shaped your perceptions of trust and love, leading to self-protective behaviors that no longer serve you. Embrace the truth that your experiences have influenced you, but they do not define you.

This process of reflection isn't about blaming yourself or others; it's about acknowledging the impact of past events on your present life. You might uncover wounds that you didn't even realize existed, but remember, this newfound awareness is a vital step toward healing. Embrace the fullness of your story, the good and the painful, for they are all part of the tapestry that makes you who you are.

As you delve deeper, you'll begin to unravel the emotions attached to these memories, finding release in acknowledging the pain and granting yourself permission to heal. The process might not be linear, and you might face moments of discomfort, but trust that you are on the path of transformation, one that will lead you to a place of inner peace and understanding.

So, take your time in this sacred process of reflection. Embrace the layers of your story and remember that you hold the pen to rewrite your narrative. The more you uncover, the more clarity you'll gain, and the closer you'll be to the liberation that comes with understanding your past.

Exploring the Root Causes: Understanding Triggers and Traumas

As you journey through the depths of your past, you may come across moments that act as triggers, setting off emotional responses that seem disproportionate to the present circumstances. These triggers hold the key to unlocking a deeper understanding of your wounds and are essential in your quest for healing.

Triggers often serve as signposts pointing to unresolved traumas. They remind you of past hurts, leaving you feeling defenseless and overwhelmed. But do not shy away from these powerful messengers, for they offer valuable insight into the root causes of your emotional wounds.

Exploring the root causes of your triggers is an act of self-compassion and bravery. It requires acknowledging the pain that lies beneath the surface and uncovering memories that might have been buried for years. Understand that this process might not be easy, and you might need to take breaks when emotions become too intense. It's all part of the healing journey.

When you recognize a trigger, take a moment to pause and breathe. Allow yourself to step back from the immediate emotional response and observe the situation from a place of detachment. In doing so, you'll gain a clearer perspective on the connection between the present and the past.

Perhaps your fear of abandonment stems from childhood experiences of feeling neglected or unseen. Or maybe your aversion to vulnerability originated from a history of betrayal. By identifying these root causes, you can begin to untangle the web of emotions that have been influencing your thoughts and behaviors.

Understanding your triggers will also help you distinguish between past and present experiences. You'll no longer react solely based on past wounds but instead respond to the present moment with greater awareness. This newfound consciousness empowers you to make conscious choices rather than being driven by unconscious patterns.

As you go deeper into your past, you might encounter emotions that have been suppressed or dismissed. Do not shy away from these feelings, as they are an integral part of your healing process. Embrace vulnerability, for it is through vulnerability that you find strength. Allow yourself to feel and process these emotions, acknowledging their validity.

During this exploration, be kind to yourself. You might discover aspects of your past that you wish weren't there, moments of shame or regret. Remember that we all carry wounds, and it is through acknowledging them that we can heal and grow. Offer yourself the same compassion and understanding you would extend to a dear friend.

In understanding your triggers and traumas, you might begin to witness the emergence of patterns that have played out in various aspects of your life. These patterns might have impacted your relationships, career choices, or self-esteem. By gaining clarity on these patterns, you can empower yourself to break free from their grip.

As you unravel the complex tapestry of your past, you'll find that your triggers hold less power over you. They transform from overwhelming storms to gentle reminders of the work you have undertaken to heal. This newfound awareness is a testament to your strength and resilience, for you have faced the shadows with courage and grace.

So, embrace the process of exploring the root causes of your triggers and traumas. Embrace vulnerability as a source of strength, and honor yourself for the bravery it takes to delve into the depths of your past. The journey is not without its challenges, but with each step, you move closer to a place of understanding and transformation.

Releasing Emotional Baggage: Letting Go of Unresolved Grief

Unresolved grief often stems from experiences of loss, betrayal, or unmet expectations. It might manifest as deep sadness, anger, or a sense of emptiness that lingers in the corners of your heart. These emotions, though difficult to bear, are an essential part of your healing process.

Acknowledge that it's okay to grieve, for grief is a natural response to loss. Give yourself permission to feel the pain, for suppressing it only prolongs the healing journey. Embrace the tears that flow, for they are the healing waters that wash away the layers of sorrow, allowing space for renewal.

You might find it challenging to let go of the past, clinging to the hurt as if it defines you. Understand that the pain you carry does not define you; it is a part of your story, but it does not determine your worth. Release the notion that holding onto grief keeps you connected to what was lost. In truth, it holds you captive, preventing you from fully embracing the present.

Letting go of unresolved grief is an act of self-compassion. It involves giving yourself permission to heal, even when it feels uncomfortable. Offer yourself the same gentleness you would extend to a wounded friend. You deserve this grace as much as anyone else.

Consider creating a space for ritual and reflection, allowing yourself to mourn what was lost or what should have been. Engage in practices that resonate with your soul – writing in a journal, creating art, or spending time in nature. Embrace the release that comes with honoring your emotions and experiences.

As you navigate this process, remember that healing is not linear. There might be days when the pain feels too raw, and that is okay. Be patient with yourself and trust that healing unfolds in its own time. Each step you take, no matter how small, is a step forward on this transformative path.

In your journey of releasing emotional baggage, you may encounter moments of forgiveness. Forgiveness is not about condoning hurtful actions or minimizing their impact. Instead, it is about freeing yourself from the chains of resentment. By choosing forgiveness, you liberate yourself from the burden of carrying the pain of others.

Forgiveness does not mean forgetting; it means releasing the grip that the past has on your present. As you forgive, you might discover that the act is as much for yourself as it is for those who hurt you. It is an act of reclaiming your power and finding peace within.

Remember that your healing is not contingent on receiving an apology or validation from those who wronged you. Your journey to release emotional baggage is a personal one, separate from the actions of others. Trust that the closure you seek lies within, and you have the ability to find it.

As you release unresolved grief, you'll notice a transformation unfolding within you. The weight that once burdened your soul will lift, and you'll find space for light and joy to seep in. The past will no longer hold you captive, and you'll step into a new chapter of your life, one guided by healing and newfound freedom.

Embracing Vulnerability: Finding Strength in Your Woundedness

You might have been conditioned to believe that vulnerability is synonymous with fragility, but the truth is far from that. Vulnerability is a gateway to authentic connection, both with yourself and others. It is the willingness to show up as you are, with all your imperfections and scars, and still believe that you are worthy of love and acceptance.

As you embrace vulnerability, you'll notice that it invites you to peel back the layers of self-protection and allow others to witness your truth. It takes courage to lower the walls you've built around your heart, trusting that not everyone will take advantage of your openness. But know that the connections you build from this place of vulnerability will be more profound and genuine.

In your journey towards healing, you might encounter moments when you feel like you are unraveling. Embrace this feeling, for it is a sign that you are shedding the layers of pain and hurt that no longer serve you. Trust that this process of unraveling is creating space for something new to emerge.

It is also important to acknowledge that embracing vulnerability can make you feel exposed and raw. You might fear judgment or rejection, but remember that those who truly care for you will hold space for your vulnerability without judgment. Allow yourself to lean into the support of loved ones who understand the depth of your healing journey.

As you embrace vulnerability, you'll discover that it opens doors to empathy and compassion. When you share your struggles and wounds, you create a safe space for others to do the same. This interconnectedness fosters a sense of belonging and reminds you that you are not alone in your journey.

Your vulnerability can become a catalyst for healing, not only for yourself but also for those around you. By showing up authentically, you inspire others to do the same, igniting a chain reaction of healing and growth. In this way, your journey becomes a powerful force for positive change.

As you embrace your woundedness, you'll notice that it no longer defines you, but rather becomes a source of resilience and wisdom. Your scars become a testament to your strength, reminding you of the battles you've fought and the victories you've won. Your vulnerability becomes your superpower, guiding you towards deeper connections and a richer understanding of yourself.

Remember that embracing vulnerability is not a one-time act, but a continuous practice. It requires gentleness and patience with yourself as you navigate the complexities of your healing journey. Some days you might feel like a phoenix rising from the ashes, and other days you might feel like a tender bud, just beginning to bloom. Embrace all of it.

As you move forward on your path of healing, remember that you are worthy of love, compassion, and forgiveness—both from others and from yourself. Embrace your vulnerability as a source of power and reclaim the parts of yourself that you had once hidden away. Your woundedness is not a burden; it is a reminder of your capacity for resilience and growth.

Take the leap into vulnerability and discover the strength that lies within your woundedness. Embrace your journey with an open heart, knowing that each step you take brings you closer to healing and liberation.

CHAPTER 4

Cultivating Compassion

The Art of Empathy: Connecting with Others' Pain

It is through empathy that we bridge the gaps between hearts, reaching out to hold the hands of those who face hardships similar to our own. You might have encountered moments when you felt an unspoken connection with someone, as if their pain resonated with your own. It is in these instances that the art of empathy reveals its profound power.

Empathy is more than just understanding; it is an act of stepping into another person's shoes and immersing yourself in their emotions. By doing so, you open your heart to their journey, acknowledging their pain, joys, and challenges without judgment. When you allow yourself to truly empathize, you create an authentic space of compassion where others feel seen and heard.

As you embrace empathy, you become a witness to the stories of others, recognizing that we are all intertwined in the tapestry of life. You understand that each person's journey is unique, and their struggles may differ from your own, yet the underlying thread of vulnerability connects us all. By acknowledging this commonality, you establish a deeper understanding of the human experience and the shared quest for healing.

However, being empathetic doesn't mean taking on the burden of others' pain as your own. It requires a delicate balance, where you offer compassion without losing sight of your boundaries. It is a gift you give without expectations, knowing that your presence alone can bring solace to a wounded soul. Your capacity for empathy extends beyond mere words; it lies in the power of your presence and the warmth of your heart.

To cultivate empathy, practice active listening. When someone shares their struggles with you, be fully present, giving them your undivided attention. Validate their emotions, even if you can't fully comprehend their experiences. Sometimes, the most profound gift you can offer is the comfort of knowing that you are there, willing to bear witness to their pain.

Remember, empathy is not confined to those you know intimately; it extends to strangers you encounter in your daily life. A kind smile, a gentle touch, or a compassionate nod can make a world of difference to someone silently battling their inner demons. You have the power to be a beacon of light in someone else's darkness.

Empathy is a skill that can be honed through practice. As you cultivate it in your life, you'll find that it fosters a deeper sense of connection with others and allows you to create a compassionate community around you. By embracing the art of empathy, you embark on a journey of profound understanding and healing, one that has the potential to transform not only your life but also the lives of those around you.

Breaking Barriers: Overcoming Obstacles to Empathy

Going through life, you may encounter moments when empathy becomes challenging. These obstacles might arise from various sources, such as personal biases, preconceived notions, or past experiences that cloud your ability to fully connect with others. Breaking through these barriers is essential to cultivating genuine empathy, allowing you to forge deeper and more meaningful connections.

One of the most significant barriers to empathy is judgment. It is natural for the human mind to categorize and form opinions about others based on appearances or initial interactions. However, these judgments can hinder your capacity to truly understand someone's struggles. You might find yourself making assumptions about their circumstances, which can prevent you from engaging with their experiences openly.

To overcome this barrier, practice curiosity and open-mindedness. Challenge your preconceived notions and be willing to learn from others' stories without imposing your beliefs onto their experiences. Embrace the idea that everyone's journey is unique, and there is always more than meets the eye.

Another obstacle that can impede empathy is the fear of vulnerability. You might have experienced hurt or betrayal in the past, causing you to build emotional walls to protect yourself from further pain. While this self-preservation instinct is understandable, it can also isolate you from the very connection and understanding you seek.

To address this barrier, be gentle with yourself and recognize that vulnerability is a strength, not a weakness. Embrace the courage to open your heart to others and share your own struggles. In doing so, you create a safe space for empathy to flourish, fostering authentic connections that transcend barriers.

Additionally, the fast-paced and often disconnected nature of modern life can hinder our ability to empathize fully. Technology and social media provide unprecedented access to information, but they can also contribute to a sense of detachment from genuine human interaction. Engaging in superficial connections may inadvertently diminish your capacity for deeper empathy.

To counteract this, be intentional about cultivating face-to-face connections. Put down your devices and engage fully with those around you. Practice active listening and be fully present in conversations, allowing others to feel valued and seen. By investing in genuine connections, you create fertile ground for empathy to blossom.

Cultural and societal conditioning can also impact our empathetic responses. Biases and stereotypes may influence how we perceive and react to others' experiences. Unconscious biases can lead to favoritism or exclusion, limiting our ability to embrace the diversity of human experiences fully.

To dismantle these barriers, engage in self-reflection and self-awareness. Acknowledge your biases and actively work to challenge and unlearn them. Educate yourself about different cultures, experiences, and perspectives, and seek to understand the historical context that shapes individuals' lives. By broadening your understanding, you open yourself up to empathizing with a more diverse range of people.

Overcoming these barriers to empathy requires ongoing effort and self-compassion. It is essential to remember that empathy is not a destination but a continuous journey of growth and learning. You might stumble along the way, but each obstacle you face presents an opportunity for greater self-awareness and deeper connections with others.

As you work to break through these barriers, you'll find that your capacity for empathy expands, and your relationships become more enriching. The art of empathy, coupled with the courage to confront obstacles, empowers you to forge a profound connection with the world around you.

Compassion for Self: Treating Yourself with Kindness

It is crucial not to overlook one of the most significant relationships in your life—the one you have with yourself. Compassion for self is an integral aspect of empathy, as it forms the foundation for your ability to extend genuine understanding and care to others. Yet, it is a facet that is often neglected or misunderstood.

You might find yourself being your own harshest critic, replaying past mistakes, and dwelling on perceived flaws. This self-critical voice can become a barrier to empathy, as it can lead to feelings of unworthiness and prevent you from offering the same compassion you readily extend to others.

To break free from this cycle, practice self-compassion. Treat yourself with the same kindness and understanding you would offer a dear friend who is experiencing pain. Acknowledge that imperfections are a part of the human experience and that making mistakes is a natural aspect of growth. Embrace the truth that you are deserving of love and care, regardless of your perceived shortcomings.

Self-compassion isn't about dismissing personal responsibility or avoiding accountability. It is about recognizing that holding yourself accountable can coexist with treating yourself gently. When you approach yourself with empathy, you create an environment of emotional safety that nurtures healing and growth.

Another aspect of self-compassion is setting healthy boundaries. As you extend empathy to others, it is essential to preserve your emotional well-being. You might encounter situations where offering endless support can deplete your own reserves, leading to burnout and resentment.

To navigate this delicate balance, listen to your own needs and prioritize self-care. Be mindful of when you need to step back and recharge, ensuring that you are in a position to offer genuine empathy when others require it. Remember that practicing self-compassion allows you to be a more authentic and compassionate presence in the lives of those you care about.

Furthermore, cultivating compassion for self involves letting go of the need for perfection. The pursuit of perfection can be exhausting and may create unrealistic expectations for yourself and others. Recognize that you are a work in progress, and that's okay. Embrace the beauty of your imperfections, knowing that they are a testament to your humanity.

By showing yourself compassion, you pave the way for self-forgiveness. Forgive yourself for past mistakes and release any lingering guilt or shame. Holding onto self-judgment can be a significant barrier to empathy, as it can cloud your ability to understand and connect with the pain of others.

As you embark on this journey of self-compassion, be patient with yourself. Changing ingrained thought patterns and behaviors takes time and effort. Be gentle during moments of self-discovery and growth, celebrating each step forward, no matter how small.

By nurturing self-compassion, you create a strong foundation for your empathy to flourish. As you embrace kindness and understanding within yourself, you become better equipped to extend the same grace to others. Remember that you cannot give what you do not have, and compassion begins within your own heart.

Choosing Forgiveness: Discovering the Freedom of Compassionate Release

Forgiveness is a profound act of compassion, a decision to release the grip of pain and resentment, and embrace the freedom of healing. It is a gift you give yourself, liberating your heart from the burden of past hurts, and allowing the seeds of empathy to blossom fully.

Choosing forgiveness doesn't mean forgetting or condoning the actions that caused you pain. It is a conscious decision to release the hold that the past has on your present. By forgiving, you break the chains that bind you to the wounds of yesterday, allowing you to step into the light of a new day with a heart unburdened by bitterness.

Forgiveness isn't an easy path, and it often requires tremendous strength and courage. You may wrestle with conflicting emotions, torn between the desire for healing and the fear of vulnerability. It is normal to feel hesitant, unsure if forgiveness is the right choice or if it will leave you vulnerable to further hurt.

In this journey, it is vital to remember that forgiveness is an act of power, not weakness. It takes incredible strength to confront the pain and decide that you will no longer allow it to dictate your life. By choosing forgiveness, you empower yourself to transcend victimhood, moving towards a place of resilience and growth.

Forgiveness doesn't mean that the wounds will vanish instantly; it is a gradual process that unfolds over time. It may involve revisiting the pain, processing emotions, and acknowledging the impact of the hurtful actions. As you navigate this process, be gentle with yourself, allowing healing to occur at its own pace.

To embrace forgiveness, start by acknowledging the pain and the emotions it evokes. Avoid suppressing or denying what you feel. Instead, allow yourself to experience the full range of emotions, recognizing that they are a natural response to the hurt you experienced.

Next, challenge any preconceived notions you may hold about forgiveness. It is not about excusing the actions or letting the person off the hook. It is about breaking free from the emotional prison that keeps you trapped in the past. Remember that forgiveness is a gift to yourself, not to the person who hurt you.

In the journey of forgiveness, practicing self-compassion becomes especially vital. You may encounter moments of self-doubt or guilt for considering forgiveness. Remind yourself that your emotions are valid and that forgiveness is a personal choice. Be patient with yourself as you navigate this complex terrain.

Forgiveness is not a linear process; you may experience moments of regression or doubt along the way. It is essential to be forgiving towards yourself during these times, knowing that healing is a nonlinear journey. Allow yourself to feel the pain, and when you are ready, choose to release it, giving yourself the gift of freedom.

As you embark on the path of forgiveness, you may discover that it is not a one-time event but an ongoing practice. You may need to choose forgiveness repeatedly, both for others and for yourself. Each time you make this choice, you reinforce the power of compassion in your life, strengthening the bonds of empathy that connect you to others.

In the end, forgiveness is an act of profound love – love for yourself, love for others, and love for humanity. By choosing forgiveness, you embrace the essence of empathy and compassion, unlocking the potential for healing and transformation within your heart.

56

CHAPTER 5

The Healing Power of Self-Forgiveness

Adopt Self-Compassion: Offering Yourself Forgiveness

The harsh voice of self-criticism often echoes louder than any external judgment, leaving scars that seem impossible to heal. But here, in this chapter, I want you to take a deep breath and understand that self-forgiveness is a transformative journey that you can embark on. It begins with embracing self-compassion—the cornerstone of releasing the burden you've carried for far too long.

You see, forgiving yourself doesn't mean justifying your actions or absolving yourself of responsibility. It means acknowledging your humanity, recognizing that you are bound to make mistakes, and that imperfections are an inherent part of the human experience. When you look back at your past with judgment, it's essential to realize that you were doing the best you could with the knowledge and resources available at that time.

Embracing self-compassion starts with gentleness towards yourself. Instead of berating yourself for past decisions, try speaking to yourself with the same kindness and understanding you would offer a close friend. You deserve your own empathy and care, just like anyone else. Allow yourself the space to be imperfect, to make mistakes, and to learn from them.

You might be tempted to hold onto guilt as a form of self-punishment, but remember, guilt only serves its purpose when it motivates you to change and grow. It's time to release the notion that holding onto guilt will somehow make up for what happened in the past. Instead, use your missteps as stepping stones to a wiser and more compassionate version of yourself.

By adopting self-compassion, you create a nurturing environment within yourself—one that allows you to heal and grow beyond the weight of your past. As you offer yourself forgiveness, you open the door to a profound sense of liberation and the potential for transformative change.

Learn from Mistakes: Transforming Regret into Growth

Mistakes are not dead ends but opportunities for growth. It's essential to reframe your perspective on regrets, viewing them as valuable lessons rather than sources of shame. Instead of dwelling on what went wrong, focus on what you've learned and how it has shaped you into the person you are today.

Regret can be a powerful teacher, nudging you towards making better choices in the future. Embrace these lessons as a compass, guiding you towards a path of greater self-awareness and self-improvement. Allow yourself to grow from these experiences, and don't let the weight of past errors keep you from moving forward.

It's natural to wish you could go back in time and undo certain actions, but dwelling on such thoughts can be paralyzing. Recognize that you cannot change the past, but you have full control over how you respond to it in the present. Embrace the knowledge that every moment is an opportunity to make amends, to become better, and to strive for a future built on growth and understanding.

As you transform regret into growth, remember that you are not defined by your mistakes. The narrative of your life is not a fixed story but an ever-evolving tapestry of experiences. Each thread of regret weaves into the larger fabric of your journey, creating a story of resilience, perseverance, and wisdom.

Embrace the process of learning from your mistakes, understanding that it's okay to stumble and fall. It's through these challenges that you develop resilience and build the capacity to rise again, stronger and wiser than before. The path of self-forgiveness is not always easy, but with each step, you gain the tools to navigate life's twists and turns with greater grace and self-compassion.

Heal Inner Wounds: Nurturing Your Inner Child

Amidst the journey of self-forgiveness, you may find that certain wounds run deeper than others. These inner wounds are often rooted in past experiences, especially during childhood. Nurturing your inner child is an essential aspect of the healing process, for it is in these early years that the foundation of your emotional well-being is laid.

Imagine yourself as a child, with dreams and innocence untouched by the burdens of the world. Now, look back and acknowledge the pain and challenges that child faced. Recognize that the unresolved emotions from those early experiences might still affect you today. By acknowledging and nurturing your inner child, you create a safe space for healing to take place.

Give yourself permission to grieve for the pain that child endured—the pain you may have buried deep within yourself. Allow yourself to feel the emotions that were never fully expressed, and understand that it's okay to experience those feelings now.

Through this process, you create an opportunity to release the emotional weight you've been carrying for so long.

Nurturing your inner child also involves providing the love, care, and understanding that you may have lacked during those formative years. Be your own loving parent, offering yourself the support and compassion you needed but might not have received. By doing so, you fill the gaps left by past neglect and create a strong foundation of self-love.

This healing journey may be challenging, as it requires you to face the pain head-on. However, as you nurture your inner child, you'll discover a newfound resilience within yourself. You'll recognize that you possess the strength to heal, grow, and love yourself unconditionally.

The Liberation of Self-Forgiveness: Releasing Guilt and Shame

As you've embraced self-compassion, learned from mistakes, and nurtured your inner child, you'll begin to experience the liberation that comes with self-forgiveness. It is a release from the chains of guilt and shame that once bound you to the past, preventing you from fully embracing the present and the future.

Releasing guilt and shame doesn't mean denying responsibility for past actions. It means acknowledging your humanity and allowing yourself to move forward without being burdened by the weight of the past. You are not defined by the mistakes you've made; instead, you are defined by your capacity to grow, evolve, and choose a different path.

Forgiveness isn't a one-time event; it's a continuous process that requires patience and perseverance. There may be moments when guilt and shame resurface, but you have the tools and strength to face them with self-compassion. It's okay to stumble, for it is through these challenges that you deepen your understanding of forgiveness and self-love.

As you liberate yourself through self-forgiveness, you'll experience a newfound sense of freedom and empowerment. No longer confined by the shadows of the past, you'll find the courage to embrace life fully and authentically. You'll open your heart to new experiences, relationships, and opportunities, unencumbered by the chains of guilt and shame.

Remember, the journey of self-forgiveness is not about reaching a destination; it's about embracing the process of growth and healing. It's about honoring your journey, both the highs and the lows, with love and acceptance. With each step you take towards self-forgiveness, you'll discover the

immense power within you to heal and transcend
the pain of the past.

CHAPTER 6

Navigating Difficult Relationships

Toxicity - Identifying Harmful Relationships

You have found yourself entangled in relationships that seem to drain the very essence of your being. These bonds leave you feeling depleted, emotionally wounded, and questioning your self-worth. In your heart, you know something is amiss, but the journey of recognizing toxicity within relationships can be a daunting one.

Toxic relationships come in various forms. Some might be with friends who constantly belittle your aspirations, partners who manipulate your emotions, or family members who disregard your boundaries. The first step in freeing yourself from these harmful connections is acknowledging their presence.

Often, it's not easy to recognize toxicity, as it can masquerade as care or concern. You may have been conditioned to believe that you should tolerate mistreatment or that these behaviors are normal.

But trust your instincts; they are there to protect you. Listen to that inner voice, and it will guide you towards identifying the relationships that hinder your growth and well-being.

Once you recognize toxicity, you must muster the courage to take action. Establishing healthy boundaries is pivotal in safeguarding your emotional health. Boundaries define what you will and won't tolerate, creating a safe space for you to thrive. Remember that boundaries are not selfish; they are an act of self-love and self-respect. You deserve to be treated with kindness and respect in all your relationships.

However, setting boundaries may come with challenges. Toxic individuals might not respect your newfound assertiveness, attempting to manipulate or guilt you into relenting. But stand firm, for this is the first step towards breaking free from their hold. Surround yourself with a support system that validates your efforts, reminding you that you are not alone on this journey.

Toxic relationships often thrive on poor communication. Honest and open dialogue is essential in establishing healthy connections. Speak your truth, expressing your feelings, concerns, and desires. Avoid suppressing your emotions, as doing so only strengthens the toxicity.

As you embark on this journey, remember that growth is not linear. There may be setbacks and moments of doubt, but every step you take towards establishing boundaries and improving communication brings you closer to a healthier relationship dynamic.

With newfound awareness and determination, you have begun to break free from the chains of toxicity. Acknowledging the harm within these relationships is a brave and empowering decision, showing that you prioritize your emotional well-being. Take a deep breath, for you have taken the first step towards building a life free from the clutches of harmful connections.

Boundaries and Communication - Establishing Healthy Connections

Setting boundaries is an act of self-preservation, allowing you to protect your mental and emotional space from harmful influences. Now that you recognize the relationships that no longer serve you, it's time to define what you will and won't tolerate.

Begin by understanding your own needs and values. Reflect on the aspects of your life that are non-negotiable and those that you are willing to compromise. This introspection will help you articulate your boundaries clearly to others.

Remember that healthy boundaries are not meant to push people away but to create a healthy distance that respects your autonomy and preserves your emotional energy. You don't need to justify your boundaries to anyone. They are valid simply because they are essential to your well-being.

As you communicate your boundaries, you might encounter resistance or pushback. People who are accustomed to crossing your boundaries may feel uncomfortable with the newfound assertiveness. Stay firm and compassionate with yourself during these moments. You are not responsible for others' reactions; you can only control how you respond.

Effective communication is a cornerstone of healthy relationships. It involves not only expressing your needs but also actively listening to others. Seek to understand their perspectives while staying true to your own. Remember, communication is a two-way street that fosters empathy and mutual respect.

In challenging conversations, practice active listening and non-defensive communication. Instead of reacting with anger or frustration, take a deep breath and respond thoughtfully. This approach allows space for understanding and resolution, paving the way for healthier connections.

In establishing healthy boundaries and communication, be patient with yourself. Breaking patterns and transforming relationships take time and effort. You may encounter setbacks or moments of self-doubt, but remember that each step you take brings you closer to a life of genuine connections.

Surround yourself with a support system that encourages and uplifts you on this journey. Seek guidance from friends, mentors, or therapists who can provide valuable insights and validation. You are not alone, and there is strength in seeking help from others.

As you progress on this path of healing, remember that establishing boundaries and fostering effective communication is a lifelong practice. It requires constant reflection, growth, and adjustment. Be gentle with yourself when you stumble, and celebrate each victory, no matter how small.

Now, equipped with newfound knowledge and a resilient spirit, you are actively shaping the landscape of your relationships. Embrace the power that comes from setting healthy boundaries and communicating authentically. Trust that by nurturing these foundations, you are laying the groundwork for a life filled with meaningful and supportive connections.

Letting Go of Resentment - Finding Peace with Difficult People

As you journey towards healing and empowerment, you confront the challenge of letting go of resentment that might have accumulated from past interactions with difficult people. Resentment is a heavy burden that keeps you tethered to painful memories, preventing you from fully embracing the present and moving forward.

Recognize that holding onto resentment only perpetuates the cycle of emotional pain. It imprisons you in the past, replaying hurtful experiences like a broken record. But you have the power to break free from this pattern. You can choose to release the hold resentment has over you and find peace within.

Understand that letting go of resentment does not mean excusing hurtful behaviors or forgetting the pain you endured. It's about freeing yourself from the emotional grip that those experiences have on your present. Forgiveness does not mean condoning the actions of others; rather, it's a gift you give to yourself, allowing you to reclaim your emotional freedom.

Start by acknowledging the emotions that arise when you think of these difficult people. Sit with the discomfort and pain without judgment. Allow yourself to grieve the wounds they caused, giving yourself the space to heal. Embrace your vulnerability, for it is a sign of strength, not weakness.

In this process, self-compassion is vital. You might question yourself or blame yourself for allowing these people to hurt you. Be gentle with yourself and remember that you are human. We all experience pain and challenges, but it's how we respond to them that shapes our journey.

As you work through the emotions, consider the perspective of those who hurt you. This is not to justify their actions, but to gain insight into their own struggles and wounds. Recognize that hurt people hurt others, often unintentionally. This understanding can foster empathy and open the door to forgiveness.

In letting go of resentment, remember that forgiveness is not a one-time event but a gradual process. It might take time to fully release the grip of resentment, and that's okay. Be patient with yourself and celebrate every step you take towards healing.

To aid in the process, practice self-care and engage in activities that bring you joy and peace. Surround yourself with positive influences and seek out activities that nourish your soul. As you cultivate happiness within yourself, you create a protective shield against the negativity of difficult people.

Choosing forgiveness doesn't mean you have to maintain a close relationship with those who hurt you. It's about granting yourself the freedom to let go of negative emotions and redirecting your focus towards nurturing healthy connections.

Embrace the power of self-forgiveness on this journey. Forgive yourself for holding onto resentment for so long, as self-forgiveness is an integral part of your healing process. As you forgive yourself, you open the door to forgiving others, creating a profound sense of release and inner peace.

As you navigate the path of letting go of resentment, remember that you are reclaiming your power. You are choosing to break free from the shackles of the past and embrace the present with an open heart. By finding peace with difficult people, you are transforming your relationship with yourself and others.

Releasing Attachments - Detaching from Toxic Bonds

Releasing attachments is a profound act of self-liberation, allowing you to break free from the chains of harmful relationships and embrace a life of authenticity and empowerment.

Detaching from toxic bonds doesn't happen overnight; it requires conscious effort and self-awareness. The first step is acknowledging the hold these relationships have had on you and recognizing that they no longer align with the person you are becoming.

Understand that detaching doesn't mean erasing the memories or experiences shared with these individuals. Instead, it's about shifting your perspective and recognizing that holding onto these toxic connections inhibits your personal growth and well-being.

Detach with love and compassion. This is not an act of revenge or rejection, but rather a necessary step towards preserving your emotional health and embracing the possibilities that lie ahead.

As you detach, it's natural to experience a range of emotions. You might feel a sense of loss, grief, or even guilt. Allow yourself to process these feelings without judgment. Remember that detaching doesn't negate the impact these relationships had on your life; it simply means you are choosing a different path moving forward.

Surround yourself with a support system that uplifts and encourages you during this process. Share your feelings with trusted friends or seek guidance from a therapist who can help you navigate the complexities of detaching from toxic bonds.

Detachment involves setting boundaries and creating emotional distance. Limiting or cutting off contact with these individuals might be necessary to protect your well-being. It's a challenging decision, but remember that you are prioritizing your emotional health and growth.

In this process, be kind to yourself. Detaching from toxic bonds is a courageous act, but it may not always be easy. You might face moments of doubt or temptation to return to old patterns. Celebrate each step you take towards creating a healthier and more fulfilling life.

As you detach from harmful relationships, fill the void with positive influences and nurturing connections. Surround yourself with people who uplift you, celebrate your growth, and support your journey towards healing. Cultivate a sense of community that fosters love, empathy, and mutual respect.

Detachment allows space for self-discovery and personal growth. Embrace the freedom to explore your passions, interests, and values without the weight of toxic influences. Rediscover the person you are outside of those relationships and embrace your individuality.

In this process, practice self-compassion. Forgive yourself for staying in these toxic bonds for too long, and release any self-blame or judgment. The past does not define your future, and detaching is an empowering step towards reclaiming your authentic self.

Remember that detaching from toxic bonds is not an act of isolation; it's an invitation to build healthier connections and relationships that nurture your growth. Trust in your resilience and know that you are capable of creating a life filled with love, compassion, and genuine connections.

As you release attachments, you open yourself up to endless possibilities. You are deserving of happiness, and detaching from toxic bonds is a powerful step towards creating a life of authenticity and emotional freedom.

CHAPTER 7

The Art of Letting Go

Surrendering Control: Accepting the Flow of Life

There comes a time when the weight of the past anchors you down, impeding your progress towards a brighter future. As you stand at this crossroad, tangled in a web of pain and uncertainty, the art of letting go emerges as a beacon of hope. It calls for a courageous act - one that asks you to release your grip on the illusion of control and surrender to the natural flow of life.

You may have found yourself clinging tightly to the reins of your destiny, attempting to mold every outcome to your will. But in this unyielding pursuit of control, you inadvertently trap yourself in a cycle of frustration and disappointment. The journey to healing begins with acknowledging that there are circumstances beyond your control, and you can choose to free yourself from the burden of trying to change them.

As you embark on the path of surrender, you'll find a profound sense of relief in relinquishing the need to control every aspect of your life. It grants you the freedom to navigate the unpredictable currents of existence, accepting that there will be storms and calm waters alike. Embrace the ebb and flow, trusting that life's currents will lead you towards your destined shore.

It is through surrender that you open yourself to the possibility of new experiences, unexpected joys, and serendipitous encounters. Instead of resisting the tides of change, embrace them with an open heart, and you'll find that life's true essence lies in its unpredictable nature.

Release and Renewal: Accepting Change with Grace

Life, like a flowing river, brings with it a constant stream of transformations. It's in your embrace of these changes that you discover the beauty of renewal and growth.

Often, change can be intimidating and uncomfortable. It asks you to bid farewell to the familiar and embrace the unknown. But within every farewell lies an opportunity for a new beginning. Embracing change with grace allows you to shed old layers, making room for fresh experiences to blossom in your life.

In this process of release and renewal, it's essential to honor your emotions, even those that may feel contradictory. You may experience a mix of sadness for what you're leaving behind and excitement for the possibilities that lie ahead. Allow yourself to feel these emotions fully, for they are a testament to your capacity for growth and resilience.

Just as a snake sheds its skin to accommodate its growth, you too must shed the layers of the past to evolve. In doing so, you'll gain the courage to step out of your comfort zone, knowing that change is an ally, not a foe. Embrace the uncertainty, for within it lies the treasure trove of self-discovery and new beginnings.

With each step towards acceptance, you'll find that the burdens of the past gradually lose their weight. The more you open yourself to the beauty of renewal, the more you'll realize that change is not something to be feared but embraced.

Gratitude and Acceptance: Shifting Perspectives on Painful Experiences

As you walk the path of letting go, you'll encounter moments that challenge your resilience, causing you to question the fairness of life's trials. However, within these moments lies the transformative power of gratitude and acceptance. It's through these lenses that you can shift your perspective on painful experiences and find solace in the face of adversity.

Gratitude becomes a powerful tool in your arsenal as you cultivate the art of letting go. It allows you to find beauty even in the midst of chaos, appreciating the lessons that pain has taught you. Rather than dwelling on the hurt, focus on the strength you've gained and the wisdom you've acquired. Each struggle has shaped you into the resilient being you are today.

Acceptance, on the other hand, is the gateway to inner peace. It requires you to acknowledge that life will not always go as planned and that certain events lie beyond your control. Instead of fighting against the inevitable, embrace the imperfections of life with an open heart. Allow yourself to grieve the losses, but also find the courage to move forward with grace.

Through gratitude and acceptance, you'll begin to see painful experiences not as stumbling blocks but as stepping stones towards growth. You'll learn that scars, both physical and emotional, carry stories of resilience and triumph, marking the chapters of your life that have shaped your character.

It's important to remember that gratitude and acceptance do not belittle the pain you've endured. Instead, they offer you a newfound strength to confront the darkness with the light of hope.

Liberating Your Heart: Setting Yourself Free from Grudges

As you stand on the precipice of transformation, you'll confront one final challenge - the liberation of your heart from the clutches of grudges. Holding onto grudges can be tempting, as they provide a false sense of power and justification. However, in reality, they serve only to shackle you to the past, hindering your journey towards healing and freedom.

Grudges, like heavy chains, keep you bound to painful memories, preventing you from fully embracing the present and embracing the potential of the future. By clinging to past grievances, you allow the past to define your narrative, robbing yourself of the opportunity to craft a new and empowering story.

To release these chains, you must face the discomfort of forgiveness. Understand that forgiveness does not condone hurtful actions or betrayals; rather, it is a gift you offer yourself. It's a courageous act of self-compassion that allows you to break free from the cycle of resentment, granting you the power to rise above the pain.

Forgiveness does not happen overnight; it's a process that requires patience and self-compassion. As you begin this journey, be gentle with yourself. Acknowledge that forgiving does not mean forgetting, but rather choosing to release the emotional burden that weighs you down.

In the pursuit of liberating your heart, recognize that you're not condoning the actions of those who hurt you; you're merely reclaiming your power and taking back control of your emotions. By doing so, you allow yourself to reclaim your energy and focus on the present, where healing and growth await.

As you let go of grudges, you create space within your heart for forgiveness and compassion to blossom. Embrace this newfound freedom, and you'll discover that your capacity for love and understanding extends far beyond the bounds of pain.

So, as you journey through the art of letting go, remember that surrendering control opens the door to unexpected opportunities. Embrace change with grace, and you'll find renewal in the face of uncertainty. Cultivate gratitude and acceptance, and you'll see the transformative power of painful experiences. Finally, liberate your heart from the grip of grudges, and you'll bask in the true liberation that comes from forgiveness.

The art of letting go is not a one-time event but a continuous process of growth and self-discovery. In each moment, choose to release the past, embrace the present, and step confidently into the future, guided by the wisdom of acceptance and the strength of forgiveness.

CHAPTER 8

Forgiving Betrayal and Infidelity

Coping with Betrayal: Finding Strength in Vulnerability

Life's tumultuous journey may lead you to unexpected crossroads of emotions, where the weight of betrayal and infidelity bears down heavily on your heart. The rupture of trust, the shattering of once-cherished bonds, and the pain of betrayal leave you grappling with a sea of emotions, questioning everything you held dear. In the aftermath of such heartbreak, the natural instinct is to protect yourself, to build walls and shields against future harm. Vulnerability becomes synonymous with weakness, as you try to preserve what remains of your shattered heart.

But it's essential to understand that vulnerability is not a weakness; it's the foundation of human connection and emotional growth. By embracing your vulnerability, you open the gateway to healing and transformation. Facing your pain head-on requires immense strength, and by doing so, you pave the way for the recovery process. Be kind to yourself during this difficult time, for the true strength lies in acknowledging your pain and choosing to navigate through it.

You don't have to go through this journey alone. It's okay to lean on your support system – be it friends, family, or professional help. By sharing your emotions and seeking comfort in the embrace of loved ones, you'll find that vulnerability shared is vulnerability transformed. In your darkest moments, remember that you are not alone, and by opening up, you might discover newfound strength within the collective support of those who care for you.

Amidst the turmoil, practice self-compassion. Forgiving yourself for perceived shortcomings and understanding that the actions of others are not a reflection of your worth can be empowering. Allow yourself to grieve and acknowledge the pain you carry. Healing begins with acceptance, and the journey to forgiveness may be arduous, but the strength you gain from embracing your vulnerability will guide you forward.

Take a deep breath, and with every exhale, release the tight grip on your heart. Understand that forgiveness doesn't imply condoning the betrayal. Instead, it is a gift to yourself – a release from the chains of resentment. As you find solace in your vulnerability, you'll uncover a newfound resilience that emerges from embracing your pain with compassion and grace.

In this moment of vulnerability, trust that you have the strength to heal and transform. You are capable of embracing your emotions and allowing them to guide you towards forgiveness. As you walk through the shadows of betrayal, remember that your ability to forgive lies within you, waiting to be nurtured by the strength of your vulnerability.

Rebuilding Trust: Nurturing a Safe Space for Healing

Betrayal shakes the very foundation of trust that once felt unshakeable, leaving you wary of opening your heart to anyone ever again. However, remember that trust can be rebuilt, but it requires patience, perseverance, and a willingness to be vulnerable once more.

Before extending trust to others, start by fostering a safe space within yourself. Allow yourself to process your emotions and experiences without judgment. Create room for self-reflection and exploration, seeking to understand how the betrayal has impacted your perception of trust. Embrace the imperfections in your healing journey, knowing that progress isn't linear, and setbacks are natural.

Understand that rebuilding trust doesn't happen overnight. Just as a shattered vase takes time and care to piece back together, trust also requires delicacy and time to mend. Be patient with yourself and acknowledge that healing is a gradual process. Don't rush or force yourself into trusting others; rather, let trust grow organically as you gradually heal and learn to embrace vulnerability.

When considering trusting others, be discerning in selecting the people you open your heart to. Surround yourself with individuals who demonstrate integrity, compassion, and empathy. Engage in open communication, expressing your feelings and concerns honestly. Pay attention to their actions, as actions often speak louder than words. Trust is earned, and as you navigate new relationships or rebuild old ones, it's essential to let trust develop through consistent actions and emotional safety.

During this phase, forgiveness may feel like a distant goal. It's okay to take your time. Forgiveness doesn't mean dismissing the hurt or the impact of betrayal; rather, it means choosing to release the hold it has on you. In time, as you witness the sincerity of others and the growth within yourself, you may find it easier to lean into forgiveness, offering yourself and others the opportunity for renewal.

As you continue on this path, be mindful of the triggers that may surface along the way. Healing isn't linear, and there may be moments where old wounds resurface. Embrace these moments with compassion and understanding. They serve as reminders of the progress you've made and the areas that still require tender care.

In rebuilding trust, you'll encounter moments of doubt and uncertainty. Remember that vulnerability is not synonymous with weakness; rather, it is an act of courage and strength. You are not the same person you were before the betrayal, and as you embrace your evolving self, trust will find its place in your heart once more.

You possess the power to rebuild trust, both in yourself and in others. By creating a safe space for healing, surrounding yourself with trustworthy individuals, and allowing trust to develop organically, you will find that trust and forgiveness intertwine in your journey of transformation.

Healing Broken Trust: Moving Towards Forgiveness

The path to healing broken trust is a courageous journey, marked by profound introspection and emotional resilience. As you traverse this terrain of emotional intricacies, you'll encounter moments of doubt and hesitancy. It's essential to acknowledge that the process of healing isn't linear, and forgiveness may not come easily. Yet, by nurturing your wounds with patience and understanding, you will find the strength to move towards forgiveness.

Healing broken trust requires an unwavering commitment to self-compassion. Forgive yourself for any perceived inadequacies or perceived role in the betrayal. Understand that trust is a delicate bond, susceptible to human fallibility. In acknowledging your vulnerability, you release the burden of self-blame, clearing the path for forgiveness.

In tandem with self-compassion, it's crucial to offer compassion to the one who betrayed your trust. This may be one of the most challenging aspects of the healing journey. However, remember that compassion does not condone the actions that caused you pain; rather, it is an acknowledgment of the shared human experience. It is through compassion that you can begin to see the multifaceted nature of others, acknowledging the potential for growth and change.

Forgiveness doesn't mean that you forget or diminish the impact of the betrayal. It is a powerful act of liberation, allowing you to reclaim your emotional wellbeing and break free from the shackles of resentment. It's a process that may be gradual, and that's okay. Forgive at your own pace, and let forgiveness unfold as you continue to heal.

During this phase, you may confront conflicting emotions – a tug-of-war between holding on to pain and embracing the possibility of forgiveness. When faced with these emotional crossroads, grant yourself the space to feel and process. There is no right or wrong way to heal, and your emotions are valid. By giving yourself permission to navigate through these emotions, you create an environment conducive to growth.

As you explore the path of healing, remember that forgiveness is not solely an external act but an internal transformation. By embracing forgiveness, you release the burdensome grip on your heart, allowing space for joy and love to blossom once more. It is an act of grace, granting yourself the freedom to create a future unencumbered by the past.

In times of doubt, remind yourself of the strength you've garnered from embracing vulnerability. Acknowledge the progress you've made and the lessons you've learned. In your journey of healing, you have the power to decide whether to carry the weight of betrayal or to find solace in forgiveness.

Forgiveness may not be an easy destination to reach, but the process of moving towards it is a testament to your resilience. Embrace the uncertainty, and let it fuel your determination to heal. You have the capacity to transform broken trust into a tapestry of forgiveness and renewal.

Accepting Renewal: Building Stronger Relationships After Betrayal

In the aftermath of betrayal, the prospect of building stronger relationships may seem like an insurmountable challenge. However, as you journey towards healing and forgiveness, you will find that renewal is possible, and trust can be rekindled in both yourself and others.

Acceptance is a powerful ally in this process of renewal. Embrace the imperfections in yourself and in others, recognizing that no relationship is devoid of flaws. Just as you navigate the complexities of your emotions, be willing to extend that same understanding to those around you. Embracing acceptance fosters an environment of compassion and empathy, paving the way for authentic connections.

As you embark on rebuilding relationships, communicate openly and honestly. Share your feelings and concerns, and be receptive to the perspectives of others. Engage in meaningful conversations that allow for vulnerability and growth. Remember that trust is cultivated through transparency and mutual respect, and by engaging in open communication, you nurture the seeds of renewal.

Rebuilding trust requires taking small, intentional steps towards vulnerability. Offer trust gradually, allowing it to grow organically as you witness consistent actions and genuine efforts. Be aware that rebuilding trust may be met with challenges, triggering remnants of past wounds. In these moments, lean into the resilience you've cultivated, drawing upon the lessons learned from your journey towards forgiveness.

Allow yourself to forgive not only those who betrayed your trust but also yourself. Self-forgiveness is an integral part of the renewal process, as it enables you to let go of past mistakes and embrace personal growth. By forgiving yourself, you create space for self-love and self-compassion, essential elements in nurturing healthy relationships.

Renewal often necessitates setting boundaries that protect your emotional well-being. As you navigate the complexities of rebuilding trust, communicate your needs clearly and assertively. Healthy boundaries are essential for creating an environment of safety and mutual respect, guiding relationships towards genuine growth.

As you find strength in vulnerability, recognize that not all relationships can be salvaged or restored. It's okay to let go of toxic connections that hinder your healing and growth. Choosing to release harmful relationships does not signify weakness, but rather, it is an affirmation of your self-worth and a commitment to your well-being.

In this process of acceptance and renewal, remember that healing is not an isolated event but an ongoing journey. Be patient with yourself and others as you navigate the ebbs and flows of rebuilding trust. Celebrate the small victories, for each step forward is a testament to your resilience and capacity for growth.

As you embrace renewal, you may discover that the strength and wisdom gained from your journey of healing serve as a beacon for others. Your experience becomes a source of hope and inspiration, guiding those who may be walking a similar path towards forgiveness and renewal.

In conclusion, the path to forgiveness and rebuilding trust after betrayal may be arduous, but it is also transformative. Embracing vulnerability and self-compassion are the cornerstones of healing, offering the possibility of renewal in yourself and in your relationships. Trust, once broken, can be mended with patience, understanding, and a commitment to growth. As you find strength in your vulnerability and courage in forgiveness, you open the door to a future where resilience and renewal intertwine in the tapestry of your life.

CHAPTER 9

Forgiveness in Times of Loss

Grieving with Compassion: Healing After Loss

In times of profound loss, you might find yourself engulfed by an overwhelming sea of emotions. The pain feels unbearable, and it seems like healing is an unattainable dream. As you navigate through this sea of grief, it's crucial to embrace compassion for yourself. Allow yourself to grieve without judgment or restriction. Each tear shed is a testament to the love shared, a poignant reminder of the bond you once held dear. Grieving with compassion is not a sign of weakness; it's a testament to your resilience and capacity for love.

The journey of healing after loss may not follow a linear path. Some days, the pain may engulf you like a storm, and other days, a gentle breeze of solace might brush against your soul. You don't have to rush the process or feel pressured to "move on" quickly. Be gentle with yourself, and allow the waves of grief to ebb and flow naturally.

Surround yourself with a support system that understands the magnitude of your loss. Let them hold space for your pain without trying to fix it. Sharing your feelings with trusted friends or family can bring immense relief. Remember, you don't have to navigate this journey alone.

It's also essential to take care of yourself during this period. Grief can be physically and emotionally taxing, so prioritize self-care. Nourish your body with healthy food, get enough rest, and engage in activities that bring you comfort and peace. Yoga, meditation, or spending time in nature can be powerful tools to ground yourself amidst the turmoil.

In the midst of sorrow, you might also discover moments of strength and clarity. Embrace those moments and celebrate the love you shared with the one you've lost. Take solace in knowing that the love and memories you carry in your heart are eternal, transcending the boundaries of time and space.

As you walk the path of grieving with compassion, be patient with yourself. There is no set timeline for healing. The waves of grief may subside, only to return unexpectedly. Trust in the process, and know that healing is not about forgetting but learning to carry your pain with grace and resilience.

Finding Meaning in Loss: Transcending Grief

Amidst the shroud of grief, you might wonder how to make sense of the loss you've experienced. Finding meaning in loss is a deeply personal journey that involves introspection and soul-searching. Embrace the questions that arise and allow yourself the space to seek answers, even if they may not be immediate or definitive.

As you go into this quest for meaning, remember that it's not about finding an explanation for the loss itself. Instead, it's about exploring how the experience of loss can shape and transform you. What lessons can you draw from this journey of sorrow? How has it shaped your perspective on life and the people you hold dear?

The process of transcending grief involves embracing the idea that life is inherently impermanent. While this realization may initially be unsettling, it can lead to a profound shift in how you approach life. Cherish each moment and each relationship, knowing that life's fragility makes every experience even more precious.

Consider finding ways to honor the memory of your loved one. Engaging in acts of kindness, supporting causes they held dear, or even establishing a memorial in their name can be cathartic and healing. Channeling your pain into meaningful actions can create a legacy of love that continues to impact the world.

Throughout this journey, you may encounter feelings of guilt or regret. You might wonder if there was more you could have done or said. Remember that you are only human, and you did the best you could with the knowledge and resources you had at the time. Forgive yourself for any perceived shortcomings, and let go of the weight of guilt.

Finding meaning in loss is not about erasing the pain; it's about transforming it into something that empowers and uplifts you. Allow yourself to evolve through this process, and embrace the growth that emerges from your darkest moments.

The Gift of Forgiveness: Finding Peace Amidst Sorrow

In the wake of loss, forgiveness may not be the first thing on your mind. However, extending forgiveness can be a powerful gift you give yourself during this time of sorrow. It's not about absolving others of their actions; it's about releasing the grip of bitterness from your own heart.

When someone you love is no longer by your side, you might grapple with feelings of anger and resentment. Perhaps there were unresolved conflicts or unspoken words left hanging in the air. The gift of forgiveness grants you the freedom to let go of these burdens and create space for healing.

Forgiveness doesn't mean you forget the pain or condone hurtful actions. It's about acknowledging the pain, allowing yourself to feel it, and then choosing to release it. The act of forgiveness is not a sign of weakness; it's a testament to your strength and resilience.

You might also find the need to forgive yourself during this journey. It's common to dwell on past regrets and what-ifs. Remember that you are human, and it's natural to make mistakes. Show yourself the same compassion and understanding that you would offer a dear friend.

The gift of forgiveness extends beyond others and yourself. It's about making peace with the unpredictability of life and the universe. Life's twists and turns can be bewildering, but by embracing forgiveness, you can find solace in knowing that you have the power to heal and grow from even the darkest moments.

Celebrating Life: Honoring Memories with Love and Forgiveness

As you move through grief and healing, you might find yourself shifting from mourning the loss to celebrating the life you once shared. It's a beautiful testament to the love you shared and the impact your loved one had on your life.

Remembering your loved one with love and forgiveness can be a transformative experience. Embrace the cherished memories, the laughter shared, and the moments of pure joy. Allow those memories to serve as a source of strength and comfort during difficult times.

Honor your loved one's legacy by embodying the qualities they admired in you. Embrace their teachings and carry forward their values. By doing so, you keep their spirit alive within you and continue their influence on the world.

Celebrating life amidst grief doesn't mean you forget the pain; it's about holding space for both sorrow and joy. The celebration is an acknowledgment of the depth of your emotions and the complexity of the human experience.

Through embracing love and forgiveness, you weave a tapestry of healing and growth. It's a testament to the resilience of the human spirit and the profound capacity for transformation that lies within each of us.

In times of loss, the journey of forgiveness can feel like an arduous climb up a steep mountain. Grieving with compassion, finding meaning in the loss, and offering forgiveness are not linear processes. They intertwine, guiding you through the labyrinth of emotions and memories.

Be gentle with yourself, embrace the waves of grief, and grant yourself the gift of forgiveness. As you navigate this path, you will discover that even amidst the sorrow, there is an unyielding light of love and resilience that can guide you towards peace and healing. The journey may be challenging, but it's also a testament to the profound strength that resides within you.

As you embrace life after loss, know that you are not alone. Countless souls have tread this path before you, and many will follow. Each step you take is a testament to the depth of your love and the courage that resides within your heart. You hold the power to transform grief into a celebration of life, a journey of love, and a legacy of healing.

May you find solace in the memories, strength in forgiveness, and the courage to embrace life amidst the pain. And so, as you embark on this transformative journey, may you find peace, healing, and the profound wisdom that comes from embracing the gift of forgiveness in times of loss.

CHAPTER 10

Forgiving Oneself for Past Mistakes

Accepting Imperfection: Letting Go of Self-Judgment

As you stand at the crossroads of your past and present, the burden of your mistakes weighs heavily on your shoulders. The relentless self-judgment and criticism make it difficult to move forward, leaving you trapped in the shadows of your past. But in this journey of self-forgiveness, the key to liberation lies in accepting imperfection.

Each one of us is human, and with that humanity comes the inevitability of making mistakes. It's time to release the grip of self-condemnation and embrace the truth that being flawed is an inherent part of the human experience. Instead of dwelling on what you could have done differently, recognize that life is a series of learning experiences, and missteps are an integral aspect of growth.

The voice of self-doubt may whisper that you should have known better, but it's essential to confront and challenge that belief. Acknowledge that you acted with the knowledge and understanding you had at the time. Grant yourself the same grace and understanding you would offer a friend facing a similar situation. Treat yourself with compassion, recognizing that it's okay to fall because rising from the fall is where strength and resilience are nurtured.

Embrace the lessons learned from your mistakes, as they serve as guideposts on your journey of self-discovery. Every error holds a valuable opportunity for growth and self-awareness. Rather than dwelling on what went wrong, focus on how you can move forward wiser and more compassionate towards yourself.

Self-acceptance is not an endorsement of your past actions but an acknowledgment that your worth extends beyond the mistakes you've made. Recognize that you are more than the sum of your errors. By accepting your imperfections, you open the door to healing and transformation.

Taking Responsibility: Healing Through Self-Accountability

In the pursuit of self-forgiveness, you come face to face with the daunting task of taking responsibility for your actions. It's a challenging and crucial step towards healing and growth. Avoiding blame and excuses, you must confront the consequences of your choices with courage and integrity.

Owning up to your mistakes requires deep introspection and a willingness to face the discomfort that comes with self-examination. Instead of deflecting accountability onto external factors or other people, look within and examine the motivations and emotions that drove your actions. Be honest with yourself and confront the root causes of your behavior.

Taking responsibility does not imply that you must carry the weight of your mistakes forever. Rather, it is a powerful act of self-empowerment and liberation. When you hold yourself accountable, you regain agency over your life and decisions. You shift from being a passive victim of circumstance to an active participant in shaping your future.

As you navigate the complex terrain of self-accountability, be gentle with yourself. Recognize that acknowledging your mistakes is a sign of strength, not weakness. It takes courage to confront the parts of yourself that you may not be proud of. Remember, self-forgiveness does not require you to be perfect; it calls for you to be honest and willing to grow.

In this process, it is essential to release any judgment towards yourself. You are not defined solely by your missteps; you are a dynamic being capable of change and transformation. Embrace the opportunity to learn from your actions, and commit to making amends if necessary. Seek to understand the underlying emotions that fueled your choices, and use this insight as a compass for future decision-making.

Healing through self-accountability is a journey that may be met with resistance, but it is one that holds the potential for profound personal growth. By facing your mistakes head-on, you pave the way for a more authentic and resilient version of yourself to emerge.

The Redemption of Self-Forgiveness: Accepting Second Chances

As you continue your path of self-forgiveness, you begin to realize that redemption is not an elusive dream but a genuine possibility. Just as you seek to forgive others for their mistakes, embracing the concept of self-forgiveness allows you to offer yourself a second chance at healing and growth.

Let go of the belief that you are irreparably damaged by your past actions. Instead, recognize that every moment presents an opportunity for renewal and transformation. Embrace the notion that mistakes do not define you; they are merely stepping stones in your journey towards self-awareness and self-compassion.

The road to self-redemption is paved with self-acceptance and a genuine desire to change. It requires embracing the parts of yourself that you may have rejected in the past. Be open to the possibility that growth and evolution are inherent aspects of being human. Just as nature undergoes cycles of rebirth, so do we have the chance to begin anew.

Self-forgiveness is not an overnight process; it's a continuous journey of self-discovery and healing. Understand that it's okay to have setbacks along the way. You may find yourself slipping back into old patterns of self-blame, but remember that each moment offers a fresh start. Treat yourself with the same kindness and patience you would offer a loved one on their journey to healing.

In accepting second chances, you grant yourself the gift of liberation. Embrace the freedom that comes with letting go of the chains of guilt and shame. As you release yourself from the burden of the past, you create space for new possibilities and experiences to unfold.

It is crucial to surround yourself with supportive individuals who understand the significance of self-forgiveness. Seek out people who uplift and inspire you to grow, and distance yourself from those who perpetuate a narrative of unworthiness. Surround yourself with a community that encourages self-compassion and offers a safe space for vulnerability.

The process of self-redemption allows you to break free from the constraints of your past, unlocking the potential for a brighter future. Embrace the journey with an open heart, knowing that your capacity to forgive yourself will radiate outwards, positively influencing your relationships with others.

Growth: Learning and Evolving from Past Errors

In the realm of self-forgiveness, growth becomes the beacon guiding you towards a future filled with possibility and promise. Embracing the lessons learned from your past errors, you embark on a journey of continuous evolution and transformation.

Each mistake offers a unique opportunity for growth and self-awareness. Reflect on the choices that led to the missteps and identify the patterns that emerged. Use this knowledge to cultivate a deeper understanding of yourself and your triggers. Armed with this newfound awareness, you can make conscious choices that align with your values and aspirations.

Recognize that growth often comes hand-in-hand with discomfort. It requires pushing beyond your comfort zones and embracing change with an open heart. Embrace the uncertainty that accompanies growth, knowing that it is a testament to your willingness to expand and evolve.

Throughout this process, be compassionate towards yourself. Celebrate your progress, no matter how small, and acknowledge that change takes time. Remember that you are a work in progress, constantly learning and evolving. Honor the journey and the effort you invest in your personal development.

As you grow, be open to seeking support from mentors, therapists, or support groups. Surround yourself with individuals who inspire and challenge you to be your best self. Their insights and encouragement will help you navigate the path of growth with greater clarity and resilience.

Amidst the pursuit of growth, remember to celebrate your successes. Acknowledge the positive changes you've made and the strides you've taken towards self-forgiveness. Celebrate the victories, no matter how seemingly small, as they signify progress on your transformative journey.

Embrace the understanding that growth and self-forgiveness are intertwined. As you forgive yourself, you open the door to growth, and as you grow, you cultivate greater capacity for self-forgiveness. The two elements become a harmonious dance of self-compassion and self-improvement.

In this dance of growth and forgiveness, you embrace your own humanity and come to understand that you are deserving of love and acceptance, despite your imperfections. You are not defined by your past, but rather, shaped by the lessons it has offered.

CHAPTER 11

The Transformative Power of Forgiveness

Radical Forgiveness: Liberation Beyond Expectations

During pain, you may find it hard to believe that forgiveness could be the key to liberation. When the wounds run deep and the scars feel insurmountable, the very idea of forgiving those who have wronged you might seem unfathomable. Yet, within this profound act lies a transformative power that surpasses all expectations, one that can set you free from the shackles of resentment.

Radical forgiveness doesn't mean denying or excusing the harm caused by others; it's about choosing to let go of the burden that weighs heavily on your soul. It's recognizing that carrying the weight of anger and bitterness only imprisons you further, while releasing it opens the door to a new realm of possibility. When you embark on the path of radical forgiveness, you step into a realm where healing and empowerment await.

The journey to radical forgiveness begins with an act of courage, a willingness to confront the pain head-on and acknowledge its existence. You must grant yourself permission to feel the emotions that have been buried deep within, giving them the space they deserve. As you face these feelings with honesty, you start to untangle the threads of hurt and resentment, allowing the process of healing to commence.

With each step towards forgiveness, you begin to witness the liberation it brings. Forgiving doesn't mean forgetting; rather, it's a powerful act of reclamation. You take back the power that was once stolen from you and redirect it towards healing and growth. In doing so, you no longer allow the actions of others to dictate your emotional well-being.

Radical forgiveness extends beyond the boundaries of individual interactions; it becomes a way of life. By adopting forgiveness as a guiding principle, you transform your perception of the world. You recognize that we are all imperfect beings, capable of causing pain, but also capable of healing and compassion. As you embrace this perspective, you become an embodiment of grace and understanding, not only for others but also for yourself.

Forgiveness is not without its challenges. There may be moments when the weight of old wounds resurfaces, testing your resolve. During such times, be gentle with yourself. Remember that healing is a nonlinear process, and setbacks are a natural part of growth. Embrace these moments as opportunities to deepen your understanding and commitment to forgiveness.

As you progress on this path, you will begin to experience the true magnitude of radical forgiveness—the freedom it bestows upon your soul. By letting go of grudges and releasing the emotional burdens, you create space for joy, love, and peace to thrive. The transformation you undergo will be nothing short of remarkable, as you find yourself unshackled from the past and liberated to live in the present.

Now, with this newfound understanding of radical forgiveness, take a moment to breathe in the possibility of your own liberation. As you carry the torch of forgiveness, its light will illuminate not only your life but also the lives of those around you.

The Ripple Effect: Spreading Forgiveness Through Compassion

Like a pebble dropped into a tranquil pond, forgiveness creates ripples that reach out and touch the lives of others. This ripple effect emanates from the compassion you nurture within, spreading healing and understanding throughout your relationships and communities.

Forgiveness is not a solitary act; it is an invitation to connect with others on a deeper level. As you extend forgiveness to those who have hurt you, you plant the seeds of compassion within your heart. This newfound empathy allows you to see the humanity in others and to acknowledge the struggles they carry. In doing so, you foster a space of healing, where bridges are built, and wounds are mended.

By embodying forgiveness, you become a living testament to the power of compassion and understanding. Your actions inspire those around you to reflect on their own capacity to forgive and be forgiven. Your forgiveness becomes a beacon of hope for those who may have lost sight of their own ability to heal and move forward.

The ripple effect of forgiveness can be particularly impactful within the context of family and close relationships. Often, the wounds inflicted by loved ones run deep, and the journey to forgiveness may seem arduous. But as you take the courageous step towards forgiveness, you create a safe space for healing conversations to occur. You allow room for growth and transformation within these precious bonds, nurturing the seeds of reconciliation.

Through your commitment to forgiveness, you also become an advocate for compassion in your wider community. The world is not free from pain, and it's easy to become disillusioned with the seemingly endless cycle of hurt and retaliation. However, by choosing to forgive, you challenge this narrative and pave the way for a more compassionate society.

Remember, the ripple effect of forgiveness is not limited to direct interactions with those who have hurt you. It extends beyond time and space, transcending generations. As you heal, you break the cycle of pain, offering future generations a legacy of love and understanding.

In the grand tapestry of life, forgiveness becomes an intricate thread that weaves together the human experience. Each act of forgiveness strengthens the fabric of our collective consciousness, fostering an atmosphere of empathy and healing. You play a pivotal role in this profound transformation, making the world a better place through the power of forgiveness.

Take a moment to reflect on the ripple effect you can initiate through forgiveness. As the pebble drops into the pond of your heart, envision the waves of compassion spreading far and wide, touching the lives of countless souls. Your willingness to forgive has the potential to inspire a wave of positive change, one that will be felt across time and space.

The Gift to Others: Empowering Change Through Forgiveness

The act of letting go is not just a gift to yourself but also a profound offering to others. Forgiveness is a transformative force that empowers change and growth, both within yourself and those you choose to forgive. By extending the gift of forgiveness, you become an agent of transformation, fostering an atmosphere of healing and understanding in the lives of others.

When you forgive others, you break free from the cycle of pain and retaliation. This act of release empowers those who have wronged you to confront their actions, encouraging self-reflection and growth. As they witness the strength of your forgiveness, they may be inspired to embark on their own journey of healing and self-discovery.

Your act of forgiveness becomes an invitation for the other person to seek redemption and make amends. It offers them an opportunity to learn from their mistakes and cultivate empathy for the consequences of their actions. Through this process, you create a space for change, not just in their lives, but in the lives of those they may encounter in the future.

Furthermore, forgiveness can help to repair fractured relationships. When you extend forgiveness, you open the door to honest and vulnerable conversations, allowing for a deeper understanding of each other's perspectives. This newfound understanding becomes the foundation for rebuilding trust and creating a stronger, more resilient bond.

In some cases, the act of forgiveness may not lead to reconciliation or renewed relationships. However, even in these situations, the gift of forgiveness remains a powerful force for personal growth and empowerment. It liberates you from the burden of carrying grudges and allows you to reclaim your emotional well-being.

By embracing forgiveness, you also become a role model for those who may be struggling with their own journey of healing. Your willingness to let go of pain and resentment can be a guiding light for others, showing them that it is possible to find peace amidst even the most challenging circumstances. Your story becomes an inspiration for them to confront their own emotional wounds and take steps towards liberation.

In a world where hurt and strife seem all too prevalent, your act of forgiveness becomes an act of defiance against bitterness and animosity. It offers an alternative narrative, one that is rooted in compassion and understanding. Your choice to forgive shines a light on the possibility of a more harmonious and empathetic world, motivating others to follow in your footsteps.

As you extend the gift of forgiveness, remember that it's not about seeking validation or recognition from others. It's a deeply personal act, one that stems from the depths of your own heart. Your forgiveness is not dependent on the responses or actions of those you forgive. It is a gift you offer freely, without expectation, trusting that its transformative power will work its magic in both your life and the lives of others.

Now, take a moment to acknowledge the profound impact of the gift of forgiveness. Embrace the notion that through your act of letting go, you become an instrument of change and healing. As you extend forgiveness to others, envision the positive ripple effect it can create, shaping a world filled with compassion and understanding.

Wholeness: Integrating Forgiveness into Your Identity

As you walk the path of forgiveness, you'll come to realize that it is not merely an isolated event, but a journey that becomes intertwined with your very identity. Forgiveness becomes a core aspect of who you are, shaping your character and guiding your interactions with the world. By integrating forgiveness into your identity, you embark on a profound quest for wholeness and inner peace.

As you cultivate forgiveness within yourself, you begin to experience a profound shift in how you perceive the world and your place within it. You no longer view forgiveness as a burdensome obligation, but rather as a liberating choice. It becomes a conscious decision to prioritize emotional well-being over bitterness, to choose love over hate, and to embrace healing over stagnation.

Forgiveness becomes a lens through which you approach every aspect of your life. When faced with challenges or conflicts, you draw from the well of forgiveness, seeking understanding and compassion instead of resorting to anger or resentment. This new perspective empowers you to navigate difficult situations with grace and resilience, fostering deeper connections with others.

Integrating forgiveness into your identity also means learning to forgive yourself. Often, we carry the weight of self-blame and shame for past mistakes, hindering our ability to move forward. However, by extending the same compassion and understanding you offer to others, you allow yourself to heal and grow. You recognize that you, too, are worthy of forgiveness and deserve to be free from the shackles of self-condemnation.

The process of integrating forgiveness into your identity is not without challenges. Old patterns of anger or resentment may resurface from time to time, tempting you to revert to familiar ways of thinking. During such moments, be gentle with yourself. Embrace forgiveness as a lifelong practice, one that requires patience and dedication. Remember that each step towards forgiveness, no matter how small, is a step towards wholeness.

As you embody forgiveness, you also become a beacon of hope for others who may be grappling with their own wounds. Your journey becomes a testament to the resilience of the human spirit and the transformative power of forgiveness. Your very presence inspires those around you to seek healing and embrace the possibility of forgiveness in their own lives.

Moreover, integrating forgiveness into your identity empowers you to break free from the chains of the past. It allows you to create a new narrative for your life, one that is not defined by past hurts but rather by the strength and wisdom gained from your journey of forgiveness. Your identity becomes a tapestry woven with threads of compassion, understanding, and growth.

As you stand at the intersection of forgiveness and identity, take a moment to reflect on the profound transformation that has occurred within you. Embrace forgiveness as a fundamental part of who you are, recognizing its power to liberate and heal. Allow yourself to fully embody the essence of forgiveness, knowing that it is a gift that will continue to shape your life in beautiful and unexpected ways.

CHAPTER 12

Forgiveness in Practice

Mindfulness and Forgiveness: Finding Peace in the Present Moment

In the midst of life's chaotic whirlwind, you may find yourself burdened by past hurts, struggling to break free from the chains of resentment. The weight of those painful memories can hinder your ability to fully embrace the present moment and experience genuine joy. But fear not, for within the practice of mindfulness lies the key to unlocking the door to forgiveness and finding peace within yourself.

Mindfulness is a powerful tool that empowers you to anchor your consciousness to the here and now, gently guiding you away from the clutches of the past. By grounding yourself in the present, you can cultivate a deep sense of awareness, allowing you to confront your emotions without judgment or evasion. As you invite mindfulness into your life, you will witness a profound transformation unfold.

Start by creating moments of stillness amidst the noise of daily life. Find a quiet space, and take a few moments to sit comfortably, closing your eyes if you wish. Focus your attention on your breath as it flows in and out, observing each inhale and exhale with gentle curiosity. As you become attuned to your breath, you will find yourself becoming more aware of the sensations and emotions that arise within you.

With mindfulness as your guide, you can now turn your attention to the wounds that have burdened you for so long. Acknowledge the pain without judgment, allowing it to surface and wash over you like waves on the shore. As you embrace these emotions with an open heart, you will begin to witness a subtle shift occurring within you - a newfound compassion towards yourself and others.

In this state of presence and compassion, you can start to sow the seeds of forgiveness. Understand that forgiving doesn't mean forgetting or condoning the past; it is a choice to release the hold that pain has on your heart. Embrace the truth that by forgiving, you are granting yourself the gift of emotional liberation, freeing yourself from the shackles of the past.

As you practice mindfulness and forgiveness in tandem, you will notice a gradual sense of relief washing over you. The burden of resentment will lighten, and you will feel more connected to the present moment, appreciating the beauty of life unfolding around you. By nurturing this practice, you pave the way for healing and a life of profound transformation.

Journaling for Healing: Reflecting and Releasing Emotions

Amidst forgiveness and healing, there are times when emotions swirl within you like a tempest, seeking an outlet for expression and understanding. In these moments, journaling becomes a faithful companion, offering solace and a safe space for your thoughts and feelings to unfold.

Through the act of journaling, you invite yourself to be vulnerable, allowing the pages to bear witness to your innermost thoughts and experiences. As you pick up your pen, you grant yourself the freedom to be authentic and unfiltered, reflecting on your emotions and experiences without judgment. Here, in the sanctuary of your journal, you can explore the depths of your wounds and the heights of your aspirations.

Start by finding a quiet moment, away from distractions, and settle into a comfortable space with your journal and pen in hand. Take a deep breath, and let the words flow naturally from your heart. Write without inhibition, allowing the emotions to pour onto the page in their raw and unvarnished form.

As you journal, you will find a sense of release and catharsis, as if the weight of your emotions is being lifted from your shoulders. The process of writing helps you gain clarity and understanding, as you unravel the complexities of your feelings. You may find yourself surprised by the hidden wisdom that emerges from the depths of your soul.

Through journaling, you create a sacred space to confront your pain and explore the sources of your emotional wounds. As you dive deep into your thoughts, you will begin to identify patterns and triggers that have influenced your emotional responses over time. This newfound awareness empowers you to break free from repetitive negative cycles and embrace healthier coping mechanisms.

In this safe haven of your journal, you can also extend forgiveness towards yourself. Forgive yourself for past mistakes, for not always handling situations perfectly, and for being human. Embrace self-compassion as you would for a dear friend, offering yourself kindness and understanding.

Moreover, journaling opens the door for gratitude and positive affirmations. Amidst the reflections on pain and healing, you can also celebrate moments of growth, resilience, and the small victories in your journey. Allow yourself to acknowledge the strengths and qualities that make you who you are, recognizing that you are deserving of love and forgiveness, both from yourself and others.

As you embark on this intimate journaling practice, remember that there is no right or wrong way to journal. The process is personal and unique to you, as it reflects your thoughts, emotions, and inner world. Embrace the spontaneity and unpredictability of your journaling journey, for it is in this vulnerability and authenticity that the true essence of healing and forgiveness lies.

Through journaling, you create a testament to your growth and evolution. As you look back on your entries over time, you will witness the unfolding of your journey towards forgiveness and self-discovery. Trust the process and be gentle with yourself, for healing is a gradual journey, and each step you take is a courageous act of self-love.

The Healing Circle: Sharing Stories and Finding Support

You are not alone on your journey of healing and forgiveness. In the embrace of community, there lies a profound source of support and understanding - the Healing Circle. This sacred space, created by the bond of shared experiences, offers solace and validation, allowing you to be seen and heard without judgment.

The Healing Circle is a gathering of souls who have walked similar paths of pain, seeking solace and transformation together. It is a place where vulnerability is met with compassion, and where the power of storytelling becomes a conduit for healing. Within this circle of trust, you find the courage to shed your armor, revealing your wounds and scars to fellow travelers who understand the depth of your struggle.

As you join hands with others in the Healing Circle, you witness the universality of pain and the shared quest for forgiveness. The act of sharing your story becomes an act of empowerment, as you release the weight of your emotions and connect with the collective human experience. In these moments of raw authenticity, you realize that your pain is not isolated, but rather, part of a tapestry of human resilience and growth.

In the Healing Circle, you lend your ears to the narratives of others, listening intently to their struggles and triumphs. As you bear witness to their stories, you cultivate empathy and learn from the wisdom gleaned through their journeys. Each tale offers a new perspective and serves as a mirror reflecting your own inner world.

Moreover, the Healing Circle provides a space for you to offer support and encouragement to others, becoming an agent of healing in their lives. As you extend compassion and understanding, you reaffirm the power of forgiveness and the transformative potential of human connection. Through this act of service, you reaffirm your own healing journey, finding strength in being a guiding light for others.

In this sacred space, you experience the profound gift of feeling heard and validated. The words that once felt trapped within your heart find release and find resonance with others who have faced similar struggles. You come to understand that your emotions are valid and deserving of acknowledgment, creating a sense of liberation and acceptance within you.

Together, the members of the Healing Circle embark on a collective quest towards forgiveness. They encourage each other to embrace vulnerability and to confront the shadows of the past with courage and compassion. As you support one another, you uncover the hidden wellspring of resilience within, knowing that you are never alone in your journey of healing.

Beyond the circle's embrace, the connections forged endure as a beacon of strength in times of need. You find solace in knowing that you can turn to this community of understanding souls whenever the weight of your emotional wounds becomes burdensome. Together, you find sustenance, love, and the courage to continue forging ahead on the path of forgiveness.

Through the Healing Circle, you come to realize that healing is not a solitary endeavor. It is a collective journey, where stories intertwine and hearts entwine, creating a tapestry of courage, compassion, and growth. Embrace this community of shared experiences, for within its sacred space, you will find the sustenance to navigate the labyrinth of healing and the strength to forgive what you can't forget.

Forgiving What You Can't Forget: Practical Exercises for Letting Go

You have journeyed through the realms of mindfulness, journaling, and the healing embrace of community. Now, as you stand on the cusp of forgiveness, it is time to go into practical exercises that will guide you towards letting go of what seems impossible to forget.

The Letter of Release: Take a moment to sit with your emotions and write a letter addressed to the person who hurt you. Pour your heart into the words, expressing your pain, anger, and disappointment. Let the emotions flow freely, unburdening your soul with every stroke of the pen. Then, when you are ready, tear up the letter or burn it as a symbolic act of releasing the hold that pain has on you.

The Mirror of Compassion: Look into the mirror, gaze deeply into your own eyes, and acknowledge the wounded parts within you. With gentleness and self-compassion, tell yourself that you deserve forgiveness and love. Affirm that you are not defined by your past pain, but rather, by your resilience and capacity to heal. Embrace yourself as you would a dear friend, with kindness and understanding.

The Gratitude Walk: Venture into nature, whether it be a nearby park, a forest trail, or by the seashore. As you walk, focus on the beauty around you and embrace the present moment. Allow yourself to feel grateful for the simple pleasures of life and the lessons learned through your experiences. Gratitude will gently open your heart, making space for forgiveness to take root.

The Meditation of Release: Find a comfortable and quiet space to sit in meditation. Inhale deeply, and with each exhale, envision releasing the pain and resentment that has taken residence within you. Imagine forgiveness as a healing light enveloping your entire being, dissolving the emotional burden you have carried for so long. Let forgiveness wash over you like a cleansing rain, renewing your spirit.

Through these practical exercises, you gently coax forgiveness to bloom within your heart. Understand that forgiveness is not a destination; it is a continuous journey that requires patience and self-compassion. Embrace the progress you make, no matter how small, for each step is a testament to your courage and determination.

As you tread this path of forgiveness, remember that it is okay to experience moments of doubt and vulnerability. Be gentle with yourself, allowing room for healing and growth. Forgiveness is not about perfection; it is about embracing your imperfections with love and understanding.

Along this journey, you will encounter moments when old wounds resurface, triggered by new experiences or interactions. In these moments, revisit the practices of mindfulness, journaling, and the Healing Circle. They will serve as your trusted allies, helping you navigate the twists and turns of healing and forgiveness.

As you near the conclusion of this chapter, take a deep breath and honor the progress you have made. You have embarked on a transformative quest, going into the depths of your soul to heal and release the weight of the past. The power of forgiveness lies within you, waiting to be awakened.

Embrace the present moment, cherish the wisdom you have gained, and know that you have the strength to forgive what you once thought was unforgettable. As you move forward, may you find peace, joy, and a heart that is unburdened and open to the beautiful possibilities life has in store for you.

CHAPTER 13

Embracing a Life of Forgiveness

The Freedom of Forgiveness - Joy and Liberation

You stand at the crossroads of a life-altering choice—the choice to embrace the liberating power of forgiveness. It is a decision that holds within it the key to unlock the doors that have confined you for far too long. The weight of past hurts may feel unbearable, but remember that you possess the strength to rise above and embark on a journey that leads to freedom and joy.

Forgiveness is not an act of weakness; it is an act of empowerment. It allows you to reclaim control over your emotions and liberate yourself from the chains of resentment. In forgiving, you refuse to let past pain define your present and future. You release the hold others have on your heart and regain the power to shape your own destiny.

It may be tempting to hold on to grudges, to clutch tightly onto the memories of those who wronged you, seeking justice and validation. But in doing so, you inadvertently grant those who hurt you continued power over your life. However, by choosing forgiveness, you break free from their grasp. You reclaim your autonomy, and your emotional well-being ceases to be at the mercy of others' actions.

It's essential to understand that forgiveness does not mean condoning the hurtful actions or erasing the memories of what transpired. It means recognizing the pain and acknowledging its impact on your life. It's about understanding that harboring bitterness only prolongs your suffering, and by forgiving, you choose to put your well-being first.

When you forgive, you open the door to healing. You allow yourself to process the pain, grieve what was lost, and make space for growth. As you release the shackles of resentment, you find an inner peace that leads to a newfound sense of joy. Your heart becomes lighter, and you can breathe again.

As you embark on this journey of forgiveness, remember that it's not a linear path. There may be moments of doubt and relapse into old patterns, but that's okay. Be patient with yourself. Healing takes time, and forgiveness is a continuous practice. Allow yourself to feel, to grieve, and to heal. Embrace the process, knowing that each step you take is a step toward reclaiming your happiness and freedom.

Now, you stand at the precipice of transformation. Take that leap of faith, and embrace the freedom that forgiveness offers. The power to liberate yourself from the burden of past pain lies within you. Embrace forgiveness as a path to joy and liberation, and let it guide you toward the resilience and strength that awaits on the other side.

Cultivating Resilience - Thriving Beyond Past Wounds

As you walk the path of forgiveness, you will encounter moments that test your resolve. It is during these times that cultivating resilience becomes paramount. Resilience is the inner strength that enables you to bounce back from adversity, to weather the storms of life with grace and determination. Embracing forgiveness empowers you to develop this resilience, equipping you to navigate the challenges that arise as you heal from past wounds.

Resilience is not an innate quality reserved for a select few; it is a skill that can be cultivated and nurtured over time. Just like a muscle, it grows stronger with use and training. Every step you take towards forgiveness, no matter how small, contributes to the growth of your resilience.

As you journey towards healing, you will face moments of doubt and vulnerability. Memories of past hurts may resurface, triggering emotions that feel overwhelming. It is crucial to remember that these moments are part of the healing process. Instead of pushing them away, embrace them with compassion. Acknowledge the pain and allow yourself to feel it fully. By doing so, you validate your emotions and create a space for healing.

You are not defined by your wounds; you are defined by how you respond to them. Resilience lies in your ability to rise above adversity and find strength in vulnerability. It is in these moments of darkness that you have an opportunity to shine the brightest. Embrace your capacity to endure and find beauty in the transformation that comes from overcoming challenges.

In cultivating resilience, it's essential to practice self-care and self-compassion. Be gentle with yourself as you navigate the healing journey. Set realistic expectations and celebrate your progress, no matter how small it may seem. Remember that healing is not a linear process, and setbacks are a natural part of growth.

Surround yourself with a support network of understanding and empathetic individuals. Seek out those who uplift and encourage you, providing a safe space for you to share your feelings and experiences. Connecting with others who have walked a similar path can offer valuable insights and inspire you to keep moving forward.

As you build resilience, you may discover hidden strengths and capabilities you never knew you had. You will find that forgiveness is not a sign of weakness but a testament to your inner fortitude. Embracing the challenges of forgiveness empowers you to thrive beyond your past wounds, becoming a beacon of hope and inspiration to others.

With resilience comes a newfound sense of purpose. You realize that your experiences, though painful, have shaped you into a person of depth and compassion. Your journey becomes a testament to the power of forgiveness, inspiring others to embark on their own paths of healing and liberation.

As you continue to cultivate resilience, remember that each step you take is a victory. You are transforming not only your life but also the lives of those around you. Embrace the strength that forgiveness brings and allow it to guide you towards a future filled with hope and possibility.

A Journey of Gratitude - Fostering an Attitude of Forgiveness

Gratitude is a powerful force that shifts your perspective from what went wrong to what is right in your life. It is the key that unlocks the door to a heart full of compassion and acceptance, paving the way for a deeper understanding of forgiveness.

When you cultivate gratitude, you begin to see the world through a different lens. You recognize that despite the pain and hardships you have faced, there are still moments of joy, love, and beauty that surround you. Gratitude allows you to acknowledge the blessings that often go unnoticed in the shadow of past wounds.

Embrace the practice of gratitude by acknowledging the people and experiences that have enriched your life. It may be challenging to find gratitude in the midst of pain, but take a moment to reflect on the lessons you have learned and the strength you have gained from your journey. Even the most difficult experiences have the potential to be teachers and catalysts for growth.

Forgiveness is a gift you give yourself, and gratitude is the wrapping that adorns it. When you choose to forgive, you open your heart to the possibility of healing and transformation. Gratitude helps you recognize the power of this gift, for it is in forgiveness that you liberate yourself from the chains of bitterness and resentment.

As you foster an attitude of gratitude, you begin to see the humanity in those who have hurt you.

Remember that every person carries their own burdens and struggles. They, too, may have been wounded in ways that shaped their actions. Gratitude helps you extend compassion to others, recognizing that they are imperfect beings, just like you.

Forgiveness and gratitude work hand in hand to create a fertile ground for empathy. When you can see the world from the perspective of others, you can better understand their actions, even if you don't condone them. This understanding opens the door to a deeper connection with humanity, fostering an attitude of forgiveness that goes beyond personal grievances.

It's essential to remember that gratitude is not about denying or minimizing your pain. Rather, it is about finding balance and embracing the full spectrum of human experiences. The practice of gratitude allows you to hold space for your pain while also acknowledging the potential for growth and transformation that comes from forgiveness.

A journey of gratitude is a journey of self-discovery. As you cultivate an attitude of gratitude, you will uncover aspects of yourself that were previously hidden. You will find resilience in vulnerability, strength in compassion, and wisdom in forgiveness. Your journey becomes a testament to the power of gratitude as a catalyst for healing and growth.

As you continue on this path, celebrate the moments of grace and gratitude that illuminate your healing journey. Embrace the practice of gratitude as an integral part of forgiveness, knowing that it holds the key to unlocking a heart that is open and compassionate.

The Road to Healing - Forgiveness as a Way of Life

Embracing forgiveness as a way of life means choosing love over bitterness, compassion over resentment, and understanding over judgment. It means allowing the lessons of your past to inform your present without letting them dictate your future. As you walk this road to healing, keep these guiding principles close to your heart.

Practice Self-Compassion: Be gentle with yourself as you navigate the complexities of forgiveness. Acknowledge that healing is a process, and setbacks are a natural part of growth. Treat yourself with the same kindness and understanding you would offer a dear friend.

Set Healthy Boundaries: Forgiveness doesn't mean tolerating repeated hurtful behaviors. It's essential to set and maintain healthy boundaries to protect your well-being. Be assertive in communicating your needs and expectations in relationships.

Cultivate Mindfulness: Be present in each moment, fully experiencing your emotions without judgment. Mindfulness allows you to process your feelings and respond to challenging situations with clarity and grace.

Practice Gratitude Daily: Embrace a daily gratitude practice, where you take time to reflect on the blessings in your life. This practice reinforces your attitude of forgiveness, helping you focus on the positives rather than dwelling on past grievances.

Foster Empathy and Understanding: Seek to understand the perspectives and experiences of others. Empathy allows you to connect with their humanity and find common ground, even in difficult situations.

Let Go of Perfection: Forgive yourself for not being perfect and release unrealistic expectations. Embrace your imperfections and view them as opportunities for growth and learning.

Share Your Journey: By sharing your experiences and insights with others, you inspire hope and encourage those on their own paths of healing and forgiveness. Your vulnerability and authenticity can be a powerful source of connection and support.

Embrace the Power of Choice: Remember that you have the power to choose forgiveness, regardless of external circumstances. The decision to forgive is an empowering act that allows you to take control of your life.

Practice Forgiveness Towards Yourself: Extend the same forgiveness and compassion to yourself that you offer to others. Recognize that you are deserving of forgiveness and embrace self-compassion as an integral part of your journey.

Embrace Growth and Change: View forgiveness as an opportunity for growth and transformation. As you release the weight of past pain, you create space for new possibilities and experiences.

Walking the road to healing through forgiveness is not without its challenges, but remember that you are not alone. Draw strength from the lessons you've learned, the resilience you've developed, and the gratitude you've cultivated. Your journey is a testament to the power of forgiveness as a transformative force in your life and the lives of others.

As you move forward, carry the wisdom of forgiveness in your heart, knowing that you have the power to shape your life with compassion and understanding. Let forgiveness be your guiding light, illuminating the path to a life filled with joy, liberation, and profound connection with yourself and those around you.

Conclusion

As you reach the end of this book, you have embarked on a profound journey of healing, forgiveness, and transformation. You have traveled through the depths of pain and the heights of joy, discovering the immense power that lies within you—the power to forgive, to let go, and to embrace a life of wholeness.

Through the chapters, you learned that forgiveness is not a one-time act but a continuous process. It is a choice you make each day, a practice that becomes woven into the fabric of your being. Forgiveness is not about forgetting the past; it's about releasing its hold on your present and future.

In understanding forgiveness, you explored the roots of your emotional wounds, unearthing buried traumas and allowing them to surface into the light of awareness. You discovered the strength in vulnerability, the power in self-compassion, and the beauty in imperfection.

You confronted difficult relationships, setting boundaries, and finding peace amidst toxic dynamics. You learned to embrace empathy and compassion, understanding that forgiveness is not just for others but for yourself as well.

Throughout this journey, you cultivated resilience, weathering storms with grace and emerging stronger each time. You discovered that healing is not a linear path, but a winding road of growth and self-discovery. It is a journey that requires patience, self-care, and the support of a compassionate community.

Gratitude became your guiding light, illuminating the blessings hidden amidst the pain. You found that embracing gratitude transformed your perspective, allowing you to see the world through the lens of appreciation and hope.

You recognized that forgiveness is not a destination but a way of life. It is a choice to respond with love and understanding, even in the face of adversity. As you practiced forgiveness daily, it became a wellspring of liberation and empowerment.

Remember that forgiveness is not about erasing the scars of the past, but about learning to wear them with pride as symbols of your strength and resilience. The wounds may remain, but they no longer define you; they have become stepping stones on your journey towards growth and healing.

As you embrace forgiveness as a way of life, you find freedom from the shackles that once bound you. The past no longer holds power over you, for you have chosen to rise above it with grace and courage. You stand tall in your authenticity, unburdened by the weight of resentment.

This book is not the end but a new beginning—an invitation to continue your journey of forgiveness and healing. Embrace the lessons you've learned and carry them with you as you step into the world with a heart that is open and forgiving.

May your journey be a source of inspiration to others, for your experiences have the power to ignite hope and courage in those who walk a similar path. Share your story, and let it be a beacon of light to guide others towards their own healing and transformation.

As you move forward, remember that forgiveness is an ongoing dance with life. It is not always easy, but it is always worth it. Embrace the fullness of your humanity, knowing that you have the capacity to heal, to forgive, and to create a life of joy and peace.

May your journey be filled with love, compassion, and an unwavering belief in the power of forgiveness. Embrace each moment as an opportunity for growth and connection, and may the road ahead be one of profound healing and liberation.

The journey of forgiveness is a testament to the resilience of the human spirit—a journey that leads to the ultimate freedom of the heart.

Made in the USA
Las Vegas, NV
11 October 2023

78923713R10085